what the book says about
sport

For my children Christine and Jonathan, whose sport has been a great source of enjoyment to me.

what the book says about
sport

Stuart Weir

Published by
The Bible Reading Fellowship
Peter's Way, Sandy Lane West
Oxford OX4 6HG
ISBN 1 84101 148 7

First published 2000
10 9 8 7 6 5 4 3 2 1 0

Acknowledgments
Unless otherwise stated, scripture quotations are
taken from the *Holy Bible, New International Version*,
copyright © 1973, 1978, 1984 by International
Bible Society, are used by permission of Hodder &
Stoughton Limited. All rights reserved. 'NIV' is a
registered trademark of International Bible Society.
UK trademark number 1448790.

A catalogue record for this book is available from the
British Library

Printed and bound in Great Britain by
Caledonian Book Manufacturing International, Glasgow

ACKNOWLEDGMENTS

Grateful thanks are due to a number of people who have made this book possible. I am grateful to Naomi Starkey at BRF for the invitation to write the book and for her encouragement throughout its writing.

During the ten years I have had the privilege of working for Christians in Sport, it has been a constant challenge to think through the issues of how to be a Christian in the world of sport. I am grateful to colleagues for the stimulation that they have provided. In particular I acknowledge the help of Graham Daniels and Andrew Wingfield Digby, whose ideas I have shamelessly stolen and represented as my own. My secretary, Helen Nunn, as always, has been a great help, on this occasion particularly on the proofreading. Thanks to Karen Avery, who allowed me to hide while writing the book and who also does a wonderful job trying to keep the directors in order!

Thanks, too, to Lowrie McCown of the Fellowship of Christian Athletes and Helmfried Riecker of *Sportler ruft Sportler* (Germany) for the help they gave in conversations and by providing me with written material.

In 1993 I wrote a book entitled *More than Champions: Sportstars' Secrets of Success*. I am grateful to the publisher, HarperCollins, for allowing me to recycle some material from that book. Thanks, too, to the many Christian sportspeople who have taken the time to give me their opinions and have allowed me to quote them.

Finally my thanks to Lynne who has not only completed 27 years of marriage to me but has remained cheerful! Thank you for encouraging me in so many ways.

Stuart Weir
Christians in Sport, PO Box 93, Oxford, OX2 7YP
stuart@christiansinsport.org.uk

Christians in SPORT

The mission of Christians in Sport is to reach the world of sport for Christ. We are an evangelical organization which also seeks to promote a Christian presence in the world of sport.

We passionately believe that sport and our love of it is God-given. Involvement in sport is therefore not only legitimate for the Christian but also a stategic mission opportunity.

To receive regular information on the Christian presence in the world of sport, plus news of sport-related evangelistic resources, contact:

Christians in Sport
PO Box 93
Oxford
OX2 7YP

01865 311211

info@christiansinsport.org.uk
www.christiansinsport.org.uk

FOREWORD

As someone who has earned his living in professional football for almost fifteen years and who has been a Christian for most of that time, a book on the Bible and sport is of great interest to me.

The Christianity that I believe in is not just for Sunday. My faith runs through my whole life. It strengthens me as a person and carries on into whatever I am doing—whether that is football or just being at home, or my marriage or relationships with other people.

Football is a very passionate game. When it is your job, it can become all-consuming. My relationship with Christ has helped me to get things into perspective. Sometimes it is helpful to see that football is not the be-all and end-all, although it is important and it is my job. By focusing on God and putting my trust and values in God, I am establishing a firm foundation. God is constant and he will be there when football has gone.

I take my standards from the Bible, but it isn't always easy to apply these standards to situations on the pitch. Football is very competitive and things can happen on the pitch in a split second that test your self-control. I believe that the Christian can play as hard and be as competitive as any other player but it has to be within the rules.

The sports media love to build you up and knock you down. One of the most important things I have learned in life is that God gives me my self-worth. My value does not depend on my performance in the last game. Football throws you from one extreme to another. One week you could be up at the top doing well; then, two games later, you've dropped a few places and might even be out of the team, so you do have to maintain a level head about it. And of course, my faith helps me in that respect.

I am sure that God wants me to be in professional football and that he has given me a job to do. Part of that job is to encourage the other Christian players in their faith. I believe too that God wants me to tell other players about him. I don't mean preaching at them. It is more just living your life before them and letting them know that you are a Christian. Sometimes a player will come and ask me a question—why do you do that? Why are you different in that respect? And you have a chance to tell them.

I am pleased to recommend *What the book says about sport* to you. It is my hope that it will help you to grapple with some of the issues that face us every week as we seek to live by God's standards in the world of sport.

Gavin Peacock

Contents

INTRODUCTION

There is a story about a group of Martians who were sent down to study life on Earth. They reported back, to the hysterical laughter of their fellow Martians, that they had seen the strangest thing.

Eleven men dressed in white formed a circle in a large field. Two men with padding strapped on to their legs and body came on to the field, each carrying a piece of willow. One of the original eleven hurled a round leather object, which one of the other two men tried to hit with his piece of willow. What made it the more remarkable was that thousands of these Earthlings came to watch this strange spectacle. Those who couldn't get there watched it on their televisions!

To anyone from outside our culture our obsession with sport would be hard to understand. However, no one from our planet can doubt the importance of sport in the modern world. Sports stars are heroes of the nation, we are fascinated by every aspect of their lives. By the millions we congregate in arenas and stadia to cheer them to victory. By the tens of millions we watch them on television. Their professional and private lives are chronicled in newspapers, magazines, on radio and television. Business loves them, because through their visibility and influence they can sell us products ranging from razors to racing cars, breakfast cereals to window frames. We admire their skill. We use the boots, trainers, clubs, racquets, balls and bats they use. We even wear the replica shirt with their name on the back. We buy the designer clothes they promote. When they speak, we listen. They are examples and role models to millions.

An American newspaper put it like this:

Athletes, their accomplishments and their private lives, are examined incessantly these days. Some people avoid the trend but it does provide a cultural service. We use sports to find some of the safest materials for talking about right and wrong, race relations and the decline of standards.

US NEWS AND WORLD REPORT, JUNE 1998

Sport affects the mood of the nation. When Manchester United won the Champions League final in May 1999, the UK TV audience was 18.8 million. Many of those viewers would claim little or no interest in football, yet they were caught up in the euphoria of the occasion. The promotion of a team like Sunderland to the Premier League affects many more people in the city than the 30,000 who may watch the team play. Many receive vicarious pleasure from the successes of their local or national team.

Beyond the millions who watch live sport every year there are tens of millions of 'couch potato' sports fans, who, let's face it, have never had a better time. Even before the digital explosion there were four dedicated sports channels available to the UK TV viewer in addition to the sports output on the mainstream terrestrial channels.

The increase in leisure time, early retirement from full-time work and the growing concern with health and fitness, has seen more people than ever before working out, joining gyms, pumping iron, jogging or even participating in fun-runs, 10K and half-marathons, as well as playing competitive sport. Recent statistics indicate that some 28 million people, half the entire British population, take part in sport or recreation at least once a month.

At the same time it has to be acknowledged that there are people for whom sport does nothing. They have no interest in the Test score, are unaware that there is a World Cup in progress. They would never be seen dead in a gym. Moreover, they find it impossible to understand how others can be so obsessed with sport. We should not be scornful of such people; we should pray for them!

That sport plays an important part in the lives of many people today is beyond question, but does it have any relevance to the Church today? Is there a connection between sport and Christianity? What, if anything, has the Bible to say about sport? Is there indeed a theology of sport? These are some of the issues which we will be addressing here.

It is the argument of this book that sport is not only a legitimate area of involvement for the Christian but also a vital and strategic sphere of ministry.

One

A Christian Approach to Sport

WHAT IS SPORT?

Sport is more easily understood than defined. Sport is a hobby, a recreation. It has psychological, physical and recreational value. It can socialize us and discipline us. It has even been suggested that the family that plays together stays together. Sport is also a job. It is big business. According to the European Sports Conference Charter, sport is 'an inalienable right of every person'.

The definition used by the Council of Europe is: 'Sport means all forms of physical activity, which, through casual or organized participation, aim at expressing or improving physical fitness and mental well-being, forming social relationships or obtaining results in competition at all levels.'

The British Sports Council has a broader view which includes the following four categories:
- Competitive sport (such as football, tennis, golf)
- Physical recreation (non-competitive activities usually conducted on an informal basis, such as walking/hiking, cycling, boating)
- Aesthetic activities (such as movement and dance)
- Conditioning activities (those activities engaged in primarily for health and fitness benefits, such as aerobics, weight training, exercise to music)

While much of this book will be taken up with discussion of competitive sport at all levels, it is important to remember that the fun-run in the local park, with its emphasis on participation rather than on winning, is as legitimately 'sport' as the Olympic 100 metres final. One event which has succeeded in bringing both together is the London Marathon in which the élite runners battle for first place and 25,000 others run for the satisfaction of participation. In the London Marathon all finishers receive a prize for their achievement.

In a leaflet published in 1991 by the four UK Sports Councils, entitled *The Case for Sport*, it is stated:

Sport is its own justification. It is a vital element in our national culture. In addition, sport:
- *contributes to greater fitness, better health and a sense of personal well-being;*
- *plays a vital part in a rounded education for children;*
- *offers opportunities for varied experiences and new fellowship in the community;*
- *offers particular fulfilment and health benefits to people with disabilities;*
- *generates nearly £9 billion of final expenditure for the economy;*
- *provides almost 400,000 jobs;*
- *promotes and enhances Britain's standing in the world.*

The cynic might add, 'They would say that, wouldn't they?' and wonder whether Britain's standing in the world has been enhanced by the hooliganism which is often associated with the national football team or the drug-taking scandals which are so prevalent today.

Few would go as far as George Orwell's view that 'serious sport has nothing to do with fair play. It is bound up with hatred, jealousy, boastfulness, disregard of all rules and sadistic pleasure in witnessing violence: in other words it is war minus the shooting' (*Shooting an Elephant*, 1950)

The Bible and Sport

If you want to know the biblical view of adultery, it is not difficult to find it. God has said it is wrong. In the Ten Commandments you read, 'You shall not commit adultery' (Exodus 20:14). The same message is reiterated repeatedly throughout the Bible. In any concordance or Bible dictionary, you can find another fifty verses which condemn adultery. It is a black-and-white issue.

If you want to find out the biblical view of sport, it is less straightforward. When God gave Moses the Ten Commandments, sport was not included. It is not even included in the Evangelical Alliance basis of faith, that touchstone of orthodoxy. The process of establishing a 'theology of sport' must, therefore, be to take scriptural concepts and principles and apply them to sport.

In this chapter we shall look at specific passages which deal with sport and try to identify certain principles. In other chapters we shall try to apply biblical principles to issues from the world of sport.

I know you have probably heard all the following 'sport in the Bible' verses before, but let us get them out of the way:

- Golf: 'I have finished the course' (2 Timothy 4:7).
- Cricket: 'Peter stood up with the Eleven [and was bold]' (Acts 2:14).
- Motorsport: 'I will return in [a] triumph' (Judges 8:9).
- Tennis: Joseph served in Pharaoh's courts (No explicit verse).
- The football team Solomon supported: Queen of the South (1 Kings 10).
- The church football team motto: 'So we make it our goal to please him, whether we are at home... or away' (2 Corinthians 5:9).
- The team manager's prayer: 'Find someone who plays well and bring him to me' (1 Samuel 16:17).

To return to a more serious view of the subject, we should note that all the explicit references to sport in the Bible come in the New Testament. The Olympic Games trace their origins back to 776BC in Greece. This could be said to be the beginning of organized competitive sport. The Greeks were very committed to physical fitness. The Games were part of their culture.

While the lifestyle of the majority of the Hebrews probably left little time for physical sport, there is evidence of running, throwing, hunting, weight-lifting, wrestling, javelin throwing and archery being practised. David would have been a hot favourite for the sling and five stones target shooting gold medal, even if Saul might not have made the javelin-throwing team. In fact, Helmfried Riecker, director of *Sportler ruft Sportler*, a German Christian sports ministry, says, 'Had David lived in our time, he would certainly have been well equipped to be a brilliant sportsman. He could run fast and had excellent co-ordination, essential qualities for many modern sports' (*Warm Up*).

In *Athletics in the First Century*, Greg Linville lists the reasons why Jewish culture took a dim view of sport. They include the association of the games with pagan rituals, the worship of victors, the self-glorification of the athletes and the worldly activities which surrounded the games. These are exactly the arguments that Christians today might have used!

In the New Testament almost all the references to sport are to Greek athletic contests. Paul, in particular, often makes reference to the games and to competition. He also spotted clear parallels between Christianity and sport, and felt that Christians could take lessons for Christian living from the experience of the athletes of the day. Paul also used the experience of the sportsman to motivate his readers to commitment to a higher cause.

Because of Paul's insights into sporting matters and his use of sporting jargon, some writers have speculated as to whether he might have received some sports coaching, participated in the games or at least been a spectator at them. However that may be, Paul—and other New Testament writers—recognized sport as an integral part of the society of their day and therefore saw it as an obvious source of imagery in describing the Christian faith. These may be categorized under the following headings:

Challenge to Commitment

In 1 Corinthians, Paul calls attention to the vigorous training of the athlete. The Christian is challenged to follow the example of the athlete and to strive for the crown which lasts:

Do you not know that in a race all the runners run, but only one gets the prize? Run in such a way as to get the prize. Everyone who competes in the games goes into strict training. They do it to get a crown that will not last; but we do it to get a crown that will last forever. Therefore I do not run like a man running aimlessly; I do not fight like a man beating the air. No, I beat my body and make it my slave so that after I have preached to others, I myself will not be disqualified for the prize.

1 CORINTHIANS 9:24–27

Here Paul uses metaphors from the games familiar to all his readers and, as countless preachers have done since, he contrasts the discipline accepted by athletes competing for an earthly prize with Christian failure to grasp the demands made on those who seek the highest of all callings. Paul urges Christians to persevere in order to gain their reward in heaven, comparing this to the athlete training to gain the prize in the games. The fact that he is addressing readers in Corinth, the home of the Isthmian Games would have meant that his readers were very familiar with the concepts he was using to make his point.

In the letter to the Hebrews, an athlete's preparation for a race is compared to the Christian life:

Therefore, since we are surrounded by such a great cloud of witnesses, let us throw off everything that hinders and the sin that so easily entangles, and let us run with perseverance the race marked out for us. Let us fix our eyes on Jesus, the author and perfecter of our faith, who for the joy set before him endured the cross, scorning its shame, and sat down at the right hand of the throne of God.

HEBREWS 12:1, 2

The image is of an athlete about to run a race, perhaps in his street clothes. Ridiculous! Runners wear but a vest and shorts, swimmers the most aerodynamic costume available. When we remember that in ancient Greece athletes competed naked, the impact of this verse is the more striking. If this is so in sport, the writer to the Hebrews argues, should not the Christian throw off any sinful activity or unnecessary earthly commitments which get in the way of giving priority to serving God?

When Charles Lindbergh completed the first single-engined flight between America and Europe, he had even torn all the empty pages out of his notebook to lighten the weight that the plane had to carry. That is the spirit of commitment that the writer to the Hebrews is seeking. It is as if the writer is telling the athlete to fix his eyes on Jesus as the finishing line and to take Jesus' example of perseverance in enduring the cross to drive him on to the finish of the race.

Tom Landry, legendary coach of the Dallas Cowboys, sees

a clear similarity between Christian faith and his sport: 'I think this is where football and Christianity have a very close relationship, because to live a Christian life a person has to be just as disciplined in the things he does as a player does to be successful in football' (in Shirl Hoffman, *Sport and Religion*, p. 126).

What Kind of Crown?

There are several other New Testament references to the crown which awaits the faithful believer in heaven. We need to understand the context from which Paul's readers would understand him. The word 'crown' (Greek: *stephanos*) was used for the laurel wreath awarded to the victor in the games.

- 1 Thessalonians 2:19: 'For what is our hope, our joy, or the crown in which we will glory in the presence of our Lord Jesus when he comes? Is it not you?'
- 2 Timothy 4:8: 'Now there is in store for me the crown of righteousness, which the Lord, the righteous Judge, will award to me on that day—and not only to me, but also to all who have longed for his appearing.'
- James 1:12: 'Blessed is the man who perseveres under trial, because when he has stood the test, he will receive the crown of life that God has promised to those who love him.'
- 1 Peter 5:4: 'And when the Chief Shepherd appears, you will receive the crown of glory that will never fade away.'

As in 1 Corinthians 9, the point being made in these passages is that the crown, which is the goal of the Christian's life, is one of eternal value as opposed to the transient nature of even the Olympic champion's crown.

Victory

There are over thirty references to victory in the Bible, including the following:

- Psalm 60:12: 'With God we will gain the victory.'
- Psalm 144:10: God 'gives victory to kings'.
- 1 Corinthians 15:57: 'But thanks be to God! He gives us the victory through our Lord Jesus Christ.'
- 1 John 5:4: 'This is the victory that has overcome the world, even our faith.'

However, almost all these references are to God's victory and it would be unwise to see in them a direct application to the world of sport.

Sporting Images to Express a Spiritual Truth

Just as Jesus often expressed spiritual truth in the rural language that the country folk of Judea would understand— the lost sheep, the sower, the wheat and weeds, and so on— so Paul, writing to people with a Greek mindset, used the language of the games.

- Galatians 5:7: 'You were running a good race. Who cut in on you and kept you from obeying the truth?'
- 2 Timothy 4:7: 'I have fought the good fight. I have finished the race. I have kept the faith.'

The application of Matthew 20:16, 'The last will be first and the first will be last' to the world of sport is less clear!

Being a Winner

If Paul had competed in the games, he would have wanted to win. He would not have been there just to make up the numbers. He had no time for accepting second best. He would have trained hard. He would have been familiar with the rules in order not to be disqualified. He would have been very focused. His mental toughness and determination would have made him a formidable opponent. All these thoughts are expressed in his letters.

- Galatians 2:2: 'But I did this privately to those who seemed to be leaders, for fear that I was running, or had run, my race in vain.'
- Philippians 2:16: '…in order that I may boast on the day of Christ that I did not run or labour for nothing.'
- 2 Timothy 2:5: 'If anyone competes as an athlete, he does not receive the victor's crown unless he competes according to the rules.'

Any sports player knows that mistakes and disappointments are part and parcel of competition. Just when the game plan was to keep it tight at the back and build from there, someone makes a mistake and a goal is conceded. The experienced player knows there is no point in wallowing in self-pity, running the 'if only' scenario. There is no point in dwelling on the past. The thing to do is to get the ball down the other end and get an equalizer. Paul expresses this spiritual thought in Philippians, but in language that any sports player will identify with: 'Brothers, I do not consider myself yet to have taken hold of it. But one thing I do: forgetting what is behind and straining towards what is ahead, I press on towards the goal to win the prize for which God has called me heavenwards in Christ Jesus' (Philippians 3:13–14).

Paul was a winner and wanted his readers to be winners too. He regarded the Christian life as a battle, as a competition. Just as a sportsperson improves his or her performance through training and practice, through discipline and commitment, so Paul wants the Christians to whom he is writing to develop their spiritual lives by the disciplines of prayer and Bible study. He wants their lives to be lived with the priority of pleasing God and not themselves.

Teamwork

Anyone who has played sport knows about teamwork (unless, of course, you play an individual sport). Teamwork is a thoroughly biblical concept.

1 Corinthians 12:14–18 reminds us about the nature of the body:

Now the body is not made up of one part but of many. If the foot should say, 'Because I am not a hand, I do not belong to the body,' it would not for that reason cease to be part of the body. And if the ear should say, 'Because I am not an eye, I do not belong to the body,' it would not for that reason cease to be part of the body. If the whole body were an eye, where would the sense of hearing be? If the whole body were an ear, where would the sense of smell be?

But in fact God has arranged the parts in the body, every one of them, just as he wanted them to be.

I once heard an exposition of this passage in terms of golf clubs in a bag. 'Which is the more important club—the driver or the sand wedge? Can the putter say to the 8 iron that it is not needed?' and so on.

Teamwork was not invented in a training course for coaches but is, rather, already mentioned in the New Testament. It was God who invented the concept. It is in this context that God gives gifts and callings to his people. Apostles, prophets, teachers, and so on, all 'play' in different positions in the team. It is no secret. In the last analysis, great victories are won by teams, rarely by individual performances.

Kriss Akabusi loves to tell the story of Britain's great

victory over the USA to win the gold medal in the 4 x 400 metres relay in the 1991 World Championships. The four individual British runners were inferior to the four Americans, but they won. As Kriss puts it, 'The whole was greater than the sum of the parts.' This is teamwork.

The Human Body

The human body is important. It is part of God's creation. The human body has been further dignified by the incarnation, when God became man and took flesh and blood. Paul wrote, 'Do you not know that your body is a temple of the Holy Spirit, who is in you, whom you have received from God? You are not your own' (1 Corinthians 6:19).

This thought has a profound influence on how we view our bodies and on how we use them. A fit, trained body can and should bring glory to God.

On the other hand, Shirl Hoffman has expressed the cynicism of professional sport as 'bodies as instruments of destruction, expendable machinery designed and developed to test the limits of expendability of the bodies of those with whom they compete' ('Sport, religion and human well-being' in *Philosophy, Theology and History of Sport and of Physical Activity*). There is certainly some truth in this view, but that is because we operate in a fallen, sinful world.

CONCLUSION

This opening review has given us some understanding of the nature of sport. It has also shown that there are a significant number of references to sport in the Bible. However, it has not taken us very far in putting together a systematic theology of sport. That is the next task.

Two

Towards a Theology of Sport

In the previous chapter we reviewed the Bible references to sport. While they will continue to give preachers excellent material for sermons at sports services, and will challenge sporting Christians to a deeper commitment, they have not taken us very far in devising a theology of sport. That is our next challenge—to develop such a theology, which is faithful to the major thrust of the biblical message.

BACKGROUND

As we have said, there is no one biblical passage which gives us a succinct summary of what we are to believe about sport. However, there is much in the Bible that is relevant to sport. Before we can understand God's purposes for sport—assuming, of course, that such exist—we need to understand God's purposes for the human race. A quick diversion into Genesis will prove helpful here.

The starting point in any understanding of God's purposes is Genesis 1. Genesis sets the whole scene of biblical revelation. It is foundational for any real understanding of the Christian faith. In the early chapters of Genesis we find the origins of the universe, the origin of sin and God's plan of redemption. We can summarize what we find there under five headings:

- Creation
- the Human Being
- the Fall
- Judgment
- Redemption

Creation

Genesis 1 reveals God as the only creator of all things. From the universe, sun, moon, and stars, down to the smallest creature—all have their origin in Christ. God is majestically in charge of the whole world. This rules out polytheism; there is only one God. It rules out pantheism; God is not part of all creation, he is its creator. It rules out any kind of dualism, the belief that spirit (or reason) is inherently good and matter inherently evil; everything that exists is created by God and is, in itself, good.

The practical implications of not understanding this and allowing dualism to slip into our thinking are immense. An imaginary line may be drawn. All the important things about being a Christian, reading your Bible, praying and worshipping God, being faithful to your church, are above the line. Below the line is everything else that isn't spiritual—having a laugh with your mates, playing sport, the arts, music, going out for dinner, sex, watching TV—things people tend to consider 'unspiritual'.

If we draw a line here in our thinking, we will despise what Genesis 1 says—what the whole Bible says about God. But in Genesis 3 we find the source of the clash between what is 'Christian' and what is 'worldly'—spiritual and unspiritual. We see sin for the first time. Sin destroys everything, spoiling our prayer life, our Bible reading. It ruins our relationships, our sexuality, our sporting life, our friendships —sin breaks everything.

When we allow God to take control of our lives, all these broken things—from saying our prayers, to making love, to playing sport—begin to be mended. God starts to address them and work inside us. He starts to deal with our lives as the Holy Spirit speaks to us through a word, through preaching, through friends; as we pray and read the Bible, he challenges us about aspects of our lives which are not right. This applies to everything from our relationships to how we play against the right winger.

Grasping this truth about God as creator and redeemer must also affect our attitude to him. If he is the creator of all things, we have an inescapable obligation to worship him in all things and at all times. In taking this on board, however, we must be careful not to slip back into any kind of dualism, separating the physical from the spiritual which could lead us to regard the former as inferior to the latter.

Genesis 1:21 tells us that 'God saw that it [what he had created] was good'. The thought is repeated in 1 Timothy 4:4, 'For everything God created is good and nothing is to be rejected if it is received with thanksgiving.' God's creation is good and it is to be enjoyed. The material world matters and it is OK to enjoy it. We are not to feel guilty when we enjoy the physical or material, thinking that we should really be more spiritual. There is no support whatever in the Bible for such a split worldview.

The starting point for any theology of sport is 'Who is God and what does he do?' If God really is the creator of everything, it is God who gives Cantona the ability to chip the goalkeeper. Seeing a footballer execute a brilliant chip can bring pleasure to God, pleasure in something that he has created, as much as any other human activity.

We must destroy the perception that sport is 'below the line' in the unspiritual category. There is no such thing as a sacred–secular divide in God's economy. All the world is broken' all of it needs to be redeemed, Christ is the redeemer and he came to redeem us. If we don't get our brain round that, we will never believe in our heart of hearts that it's really OK to devote time to sport.

The Human Being

Genesis also helps us with the question 'Who or what is a human being and what is the meaning of life?' Genesis 1:26 gives us the answer, 'Then God said, "Let us make man in our image, in our likeness and let them rule over the fish of the sea and the birds of the air, over the livestock, over all the earth and over all the creatures that move along the ground."'

Humans are made in God's image and appointed as his ruling representatives on earth, sharing God's divine rule. The work assigned to us gives us dignity. There is scope for creativity and fulfilment. Leonard Browne, in his book *Sport and Recreation and Evangelism in the Local Church*, quotes *At Work and at Play* (Frey et al., Paideia Press, p. 42) that 'God created man with a desire to play'.

If men and women are truly made in the image of God as Genesis says, this gives people a unique integral value. It does not depend on what we can do but on what we already are. Our value derives from our relationship with God. We are freed from a self-image which depends on our performance in our last game.

The Fall

Sin entered into the equation in Genesis 3 when Adam and Eve chose to rebel against God's authority. Not satisfied with being made in the image of God, they wanted more. They wanted to be like God. The Bible tells us (in Romans 5, for example) that Adam and Eve's sin affects us all—we are all sinners because of them. Yet at the same time, by personal choice we perpetuate sin and become responsible for our own actions. The whole of creation is tarnished. What God created for us to enjoy is now ruined by our selfish and sinful attitude to it. Work, for example, is now less about creativity and dignity than tedious effort and frustration.

Judgment

The consequence of the fall is judgment. In Genesis 3:14 God says, 'Because you have done this…' and continues to outline for the serpent, Adam and Eve the consequences of their actions. Another example is God's destruction of sinful humanity in the flood in Genesis 6. God's anger and judgment make us uncomfortable but they are an integral part of the Bible story.

Redemption

God did not wipe out the whole of humanity with the flood. Noah and his family were saved. This story has a significance beyond its historical context. It is a symbol of what God is going to do in the future at the end of the world when he will judge everyone. It is also pointing forward to the great salvation which will come to the world in Christ. In Christ, God's perfect man, creation is restored. The human race comes into its true state only through a relationship with Jesus Christ both in this life and, ultimately, in heaven for ever.

All aspects of our lives are involved in our relationship with Christ and restored by it—our religion, our family, our work, our hobbies—everything. We are saved to represent Christ in all things at all times.

Now how does all this apply to sport?

ARGUMENT FROM SILENCE

Theology based on an 'argument from silence' (meaning that because a particular activity is not mentioned in the Bible, an assumption is made about it) is always somewhat suspect. However, on this occasion it is a good starting point as we move into the task of defining a theology of sport.

As we have seen already, the New Testament writers use a number of sports illustrations. In none of these is there an explicit or implicit condemnation of sporting competition. If indeed sport is evil, it is surprising that the Holy Spirit, who inspired the scriptures, did not lead the writers to omit the sporting metaphors or indeed to warn their readers of the dangers of having anything to do with the games.

It is, without question, a reasonable starting point in our quest for a biblical attitude to sport to conclude that there are absolutely no grounds for seeing the Bible as anti-sport.

Going back to our understanding of creation, this conclusion is exactly what we would have expected.

A GIFT FROM GOD

The evidence suggests that sport is a gift from God. As we have seen, sport and our ability to play and enjoy it are part of God's creation. As we have also already seen, the Bible shows none of the body–soul dualism found in Greek thought. The human body is a unity, and the Bible has a high view of the human body.

The Bible reveals a God who gives gifts to men and women. There are spiritual gifts as well as natural and physical abilities. All of them are from God and are to be used for our enjoyment and God's glory. It would be a perverse interpretation of the Bible to argue—as some do—that some gifts, like a musical talent, are from God, whereas speed, co-ordination and other sporting talents are not. Sporting ability is as much a gift from God as singing in the choir or Sunday School teaching. All are capable of being used in God's service for his glory.

World-record holder in the triple jump, Jonathan Edwards, puts it well when he says, 'The fact that the human body can jump 18.29 metres is testimony to what a great God we serve.'

Similarly, golfer Bernhard Langer, in his speech following a victory, will often thank God for 'a beautiful world in which to play golf, and the ability to play the game'. Many of us can identify with those sentiments, though perhaps the first half more than the second!

Peter Pollock, former South African fast bowler, makes a helpful distinction when he says, 'Ability is a gift from God but lust for success was not his plan' ('The myth of success', in *Today*, September 1999).

When sportspeople recognize their sporting ability as a gift from God, they are set free to enjoy it and to use it for his glory. Gone are the guilt feelings that sport is unholy or, at best, a tolerable but low-priority activity. They can go out and play their sport to the best of their ability, in the spirit of Paul in Colossians 3:23: 'Whatever you do, work at it with all your heart, as working for the Lord, not for men.' The individual ought to feel the freedom to be a sportsperson and to demonstrate his or her relationship with a life-changing, sin-conquering God and to declare faith in that God in the sporting environment.

It is a Christian responsibility to give a lead to society as to how God's gift of sport is to be used.

AN OPPORTUNITY FOR WORSHIP

A definition of worship as an activity that we practise on a Sunday morning between 10.30 and 11.30, mainly through singing 'worship' songs, is inadequate. Of course, corporate public worship is an important part of our spiritual lives. However, the biblical view of worship is a seven-days-a-week lifestyle activity, rather than requiring but one hour on a Sunday morning. This point is made clearly in Romans 12:1: 'Therefore I urge you, brothers, in view of God's mercy, to offer your bodies as living sacrifices, holy and pleasing to God—this is your spiritual act of worship.' We are to worship God and represent Christ all the time in all things. That is, everything in life is to be an act of worship to God. It is a million miles from the religion of 'keep Sunday holy and do what you like the rest of the week'. The Christian is to please God in everything, by doing it as if for God. That includes sport. Jonathan Edwards can worship the creator by training and fine-tuning his body to the point where it can triple-jump 18.29 metres. Others can worship God with more humble performances if their attitude and motivation are to glorify God.

This thought is well encapsulated in the scene from the film *Chariots of Fire*, when Eric Liddell's thoughts as he runs are, 'God made me for a purpose, but he also made me fast and when I run, I feel his pleasure.' More and more Christians have come to see sport, played with the right attitude, as something that can bring pleasure to God.

Those twenty words from *Chariots of Fire* are very familiar but how many people know how the quotation continues? The full quotation is, 'I believe God made me for a purpose —for China—but when I run I feel his pleasure and to give it up would be to hold him in contempt. To win is to honour him.' In the second sentence, the idea is that not to use the talent he has been given would be to dishonour God.

This may seem a convenient way of justifying playing sport all day long—as an opportunity to worship God! Of course, there must be moderation and balance in all things.

That certainly rings true for Gavin Peacock, professional footballer with Newcastle United, Chelsea and Queen's Park Rangers:

I regard my ability to play football as a gift from God. He has given me the talent. I believe he wants me to work hard and make the best of what he has given me and use it to his glory. I love that moment in Chariots of Fire *when Eric Liddell says, 'God made me for a purpose…' I wouldn't put it as poetically as that, but when I play I am aware of God's presence and try to give him the glory whether it goes well or badly. I believe that anything beautiful—whether it is lovely scenery or a sporting skill executed perfectly—is a reflection of the creator. Sometimes during a game you just strike the ball perfectly—like a goal I scored for Chelsea against Swindon [which was disallowed because someone else was offside]. Sometimes everything just comes together and what you try comes off. It seems a real God-given moment that you couldn't repeat if you tried. I also feel thankful to God when it happens.*

Al Kennedy, who played rugby for Cambridge University, also echoes Eric Liddell: 'I think of every part of my life as being Christian. God has made me with the gifts I have. I do feel his pleasure when I kick a goal.'

Again Peter Pollock has a useful insight on this issue: 'How you handle fame, success and failure and your perspective on life, is what glorifies God, not the trophies and prizes and acclamation' ('The myth of success').

According to the Westminster Confession, we were created to glorify God. Is there any reason why that should not be on the sports field just as much as in a church?

AN OPPORTUNITY TO
LOVE ONE'S NEIGHBOUR

The words of Jesus, 'Love your neighbour as yourself' (Matthew 22:39) represent a significant challenge to us as we play competitive sport. In a culture where hating an opponent may be considered the norm, we are to see our opponent as a neighbour and to love her or him. We are to see God in the joy of companionship and competition that we find in sport.

Working out the challenge of loving our opponent in the hurly-burly of competitive sport is considered in more detail in Chapter 5, 'Does God Care Who Wins?' Suffice it to say here that whether or not God cares who wins, he certainly does care how we treat our opponent.

A TESTING GROUND

God's purpose for his followers is that they should live godly lives, which please him, wherever they find themselves. They are to follow Jesus' instruction to 'let your light shine before men, that they may see your good deeds and praise your Father in heaven' (Matthew 5:16).

The heat of the moment on the sports field is a stern test for the Christian. Can you forgive the opponent who has just fouled you? Can you avoid resenting the opponent who has cheated and got away with it and so beaten you? Sport can be a crucible in which your faith is tested in the flames of competition. In fact Alvin Schindel, quoted by Larry Matthews in *Faith Today* (Canada's evangelical news and feature magazine, November/December 1995), suggests that sports 'teach us we should do what we can get away with'.

A sign to the world that we belong to Jesus and there is authenticity in our message lies in the demonstration of a life in submission to our Master, reflecting genuine love and forgiveness, especially in the difficult times we all experience in sport.

As we noticed above, there are many similarities between sport and the Christian life and many things we can learn from sport and apply to our Christian life. There is, too, the character-building aspect of sport. What Paul called 'working out your own salvation' (Philippians 2:12) on the sports field, and knowing how to react to difficult situations, can strengthen one's faith enormously.

The Samoan rugby player, Va'aiga Tuigamala, who has enjoyed success with the New Zealand All Blacks, Wigan Rugby League Club and the Newcastle Falcons, has an interesting perspective on the issue:

I have learned that my witness has been a blessing for me and not only for me but to a lot of other players. They see me as the gentle giant but they also know that if anyone crosses me I am more than happy to take the game into my own hands and make the most of it. That's not going out and belting someone. But whatever I do, I get my own back by running straight and hard and, if they get the ball, making sure that I tackle hard, within the rules. God wants you to go out there and be a warrior, be a soldier, and some of the players have responded tremendously. I remember when I first came over here [to England], I used to get beaten up, and my wife will testify to this—that I used to come home every week with a black eye, cuts to the face and bruises to the body, done deliberately.

I cried to the Lord, 'What do I do? Do I retaliate?' But he said, 'No, No, No. Just stay focused and I'll handle everything.' And the guys who were beating me up when I first came, they are the same guys who are able to come up and shake my hands. They now thank me for the game and say, 'Well played!' And it's tremendous to have that kind of influence for they know I'm not that sort of person. I can take a lot but I'm not willing to give a lot as well.

I think a lot of it has to come down to God allowing me to be so focused, to control myself and it's certainly from God's influence as well.

Adrian Davies' great ambition was to play for Wales in the Rugby World Cup. He achieved the ambition. As a Christian he committed it to God, but it did not work out as he would have hoped:

I have such contrasting memories of the 1995 World Cup. The most vivid memory is the dressing room after the 24–23 defeat by Ireland. It is the most disappointed dressing room I have ever been in. There was just an overwhelming sense of disappointment and that we had not done ourselves justice. We all knew that we should have won the match.

I had been waiting to play in a game of that importance for the six years I had been in the Welsh squad. I prayed in the shower, before the game, but then things didn't work out. Afterwards I did ask God why, and I don't really know the answer even now.

C.T. Studd gave up a promising future in international cricket to become a missionary in China at the end of the nineteenth century. In his biography of Studd, Norman Grubb wrote, 'C.T. never regretted that he played cricket… for by applying himself to the game he learned lessons of courage, self-denial and endurance which, after his life had been fully consecrated to Christ, were used in his service' (*C.T. Studd*, p. 31).

AN OPPORTUNITY FOR WITNESS

Part of God's plan for his servants is that they should fulfil the great commission of Matthew 28:19, 'Therefore go and make disciples of all nations, baptizing them in the name of the Father and of the Son and of the Holy Spirit.'

This is reiterated in Acts 1:8: 'But you will receive power when the Holy Spirit comes on you; and you will be my witnesses in Jerusalem, and in all Judea and Samaria, and to the ends of the earth.'

In 2 Corinthians 5:20 Paul describes Christians as 'Christ's ambassadors'. For the sportsperson, the sphere in which one is likely to be most effective as an ambassador is in sport. It is a wonderful way of making friends and spending time with people, and friends are the people who are most likely to trust our opinions and listen to us.

We are all called to be witnesses where God has placed us. Every situation has its own difficulties. Sportspeople have the opportunity to demonstrate the image of God in an environment which is often lacking in sacrificial and unconditional love.

Nduka Odizor, a quarter-finalist at Wimbledon in the early 1980s, was able to witness to an opponent in a very practical way. 'The Duke' takes up the story:

I was playing the qualifying round of a grass tournament in Holland when I noticed my next opponent was upset about something. I overheard him say that he had been unable to get a pair of grass court shoes and as a result he was slipping all over the place. I offered to lend him a pair of mine. My opponent's face dropped in astonishment. The thought, 'How could anyone be so stupid?' was written all over his face. 'Here's my hotel key,' I said, 'if you want to go and get them or send someone for them.'

When our match was called, there he was, wearing my shoes! He won the first set, but I came back to win the next two. At the end he couldn't say thank you enough. He was so sincere. Nothing like this had ever happened to him before.

'SERVING TO WIN', TENNIS MINISTRY NEWLETTER, FALL 1990

Christians have found opportunities to share the gospel in gyms, on golf courses, tennis courts and sports fields the world over. The lost may not come to church but, by seeing the sports club as your mission-field, you can take Christ to them.

Dr Eddie Fox of the United Methodist Church World Evangelism Council has said, 'Just as the roads of Rome were utilized as bridges for the gospel to the ancient world, so sports, in this era, provide unique intersections in the world for the witness of Christ.'

Hansie Cronje, captain of the South African team, is conscious of the opportunity that his involvement in Test cricket brings. He says:

I'm not going out there praying, 'Please help me to win', but I go to glorify his name and hopefully, when you do get the opportunity in front of crowds and people, just to say the odd word that you are a Christian and you do believe in God and you appreciate what Jesus has done for you and what he can do for somebody else.

IMPORTANT BUT NOT ALL-IMPORTANT

Paul wrote to Timothy, 'For physical training is of some value, but godliness has value for all things, holding promise for both the present life and the life to come' (1 Timothy 4:8). Sport is legitimate. It is part of God's creation and it brings pleasure to many. It is as worthwhile a part of human activity as any other. As seen above, through sport people can glorify God and it can provide opportunities for outreach. However, at the end of the day, sport is transient. It is, like all other human activity, going to pass away. In the light of eternity it is of limited value.

Sport, in and of itself, is not an end but a means to an end. Sport is a way to know and grow in Christ. While there is a danger of sport becoming an idol if it is put ahead of Christ, sport is important as long as it is the arena in which we serve Christ.

Helmfried Riecker expresses it thus in his book *Warm Up*:

The New Testament writers are unanimous, not only about the hope of eternal life after death, but also that the goal of that eternal life is to be with Christ in the presence of God the Father... It is great to set sports goals and to gain a real part of your meaning in life through the fulfilment of these goals. However, the short-term goals will appear in a different perspective when you see again the real goal of your life. If winning a final is an exciting thing, how much greater will be the celebration of the ultimate goal of your life?

Peter Pollock would agree with that: 'As Christian sportsmen our task is to throw ourselves wholeheartedly into applying the gifts God has given us in the arena he has prepared for us, realizing always that the final victory isn't the World Cup' ('The myth of success').

While it is a great and quotable line, the Christian must say quite simply that Bill Shankly was wrong in his view—if, in reality, he really believed it—that 'football is not a matter of life and death; it is more important than that'. However, as an example of the passions that sport can arouse, football was a matter of life and death for Andres Escobar, the Columbian player who was murdered in 1994 after scoring an own goal in the World Cup.

Alex Ribeiro's telegraph to a number of players like Cesar Sampaio and Cleber, who would have been disappointed not to have been selected for the 1994 Brazil World Cup squad, makes this point well:

At first we were sad not to see your name on Coach Parreira's list. Then we remembered that everything works together for good to those who love God. This promise includes you, even though you weren't picked this time. May our Great Comforter strengthen your heart with the assurance that your name is included on another list—the one in the Book of Life. You are a 'draft pick' to spend eternity with God.

WHO WON THE WORLD CUP?, P. 30

David Hewitt, international rugby player in the 1950s–60s, writing a comparison of rugby in his day with the game in 1999, ended with these words: 'But I do hope those who play and control it today will never forget it is only a game (OK, it is only a job), that winning is not everything, that friendships will outlast the thrill of victory, and that sportsmanship is still valued' (*On the Winning Side*, CPO).

A PERSON'S SIGNIFICANCE IS NOT BASED ON SPORTING ACHIEVEMENT

A common cliché in sport is that you are 'only as good as your last game'. If your significance and self-worth are determined by your last performance on the sports field, then you have a problem. Even the greatest of sportspeople cannot achieve to the same standard all the time. Champion golfer Bernhard Langer has said that he is dissatisfied with 95% of the golf shots that he hits—and he is a winner! What hope is there for you and me?

When footballer Alan Comfort's career was ended by injury, this was a problem for him.

You go from being worth an awful lot to people to absolutely nothing. When you begin to realize that, your self-respect just falls apart. You are nothing. You're less than that… From a Christian point of view it was always helpful to think that God knew why it was happening and that God was still in control.

The difficulty inherent in seeking your self-worth from your sporting achievement is well put by former US Master's winner, Larry Mize:

If my job or my performance is what makes me significant then my life will be like a rollercoaster. If I play well, I'm happy. If I play bad, I'll be upset and I won't be happy until I play good again. I don't want to live like that and thankfully I don't have to. I have infinite worth because God sent his only Son, Jesus Christ, to die for me. Isn't that truly significant?'

LINKS LETTER LEAFLET

Gavin Peacock is another who has learned not to depend on sporting success for satisfaction:

That is the thing about football. You have got to keep a level head. If you do get carried away, football throws you from one extreme to another. Within a week you could be up at the top doing well, then two games later, the next weekend, you've dropped a few places or you might be out of the team. So you do have to maintain a level head about it. And of course, my faith helps me in that respect. It is God who gives me my self-worth, my value first, so I am a Christian first and then I am a footballer.

The highlight of Gavin's footballing career was to play in the FA Cup Final for Chelsea against Manchester United in 1994. It was a great experience, the fulfilment of a lifetime dream. It could have been better as Gavin's shot hit the bar when the score was 0–0. Yet Gavin feels now that if he had been looking for his significance in life in that game, he would have been disappointed: 'Beforehand I thought, just to play in the Cup Final, that would be great for me even if I did not win it. But then you play in it and it's gone. If that is just what you are hanging your hopes on, any success is just momentary.'

In the ups and downs of sporting life, it is essential to put your faith in somebody who does not only love you when you play well: 'Jesus Christ… the same yesterday and today and for ever' (Hebrews 13:8). If your self-worth is based on an eternal relationship with Jesus Christ, then you can play sport with all your might, give it everything, yet know that ultimately it is not in sport alone that you find your significance.

Bernhard Langer is one who would echo that thought.

I realized when I was about 28 years old and I had basically achieved almost everything that I wanted to and dreamed of—I realized that material things don't make you happy. There had to be more in this life than just accumulating money in the bank or cars or houses or whatever. You just want more, more, more and are never satisfied. Through a Bible study on the US Tour, I came to know Jesus Christ as my personal saviour and that made all the difference.

Peter Pollock is even more blunt: 'The need to succeed to be happy is a one-way ticket to depression' ('The myth of success').

It is important always to remember that our identity as Christians comes from the fact that God has created us in his own image and that through Christ he has redeemed us. Genesis 2:25 states that Adam and Eve 'were both naked and they felt no shame'. When they sinned (Genesis 3), they realized that they were naked, and sewed leaves together to cover themselves. They were ashamed of who they were. In our fallen world, people often seek their identity in another facet of creation—work, achievement or sport—because they are ashamed of who they are.

As we continue through the book we will see how these principles can be applied to sporting situations, at all levels and in different sports.

SUMMARY

Any theology of sport must include these elements. Sport is:

- a gift from God
- part of God's creation
- an opportunity for worship
- an opportunity to love one's neighbour
- a testing ground
- an opportunity for witness
- important but not all-important
- **not the source of our significance as people**

Three

Using Time Profitably

The Christian Church has, over the years, had an ambivalent attitude to sport. Originating in the philosophy of J.J. Rousseau, the doctrine of 'muscular Christianity' became influential in the last century. This was a view that there was positive moral influence in physical exercise and sport and that competitive sport had an ethical basis; training in moral behaviour on the playing field was transferable to the outside world. 'Unselfishness, justice, health: these were the type of ideals that were manifest in sport, but also in any proper Christian society' (Peter McIntosh, *Fair Play*, Heinemann, 1979).

Manifestations of muscular Christianity included the development of sport in public schools and the encouragement of football among the working classes. In fact, something like a quarter of today's English professional football teams were founded by churches—for example, Queens Park Rangers was originally 'St Jude's', Southampton started life as 'Southampton St Mary' and Fulham as 'Fulham St Andrew's'.

In later years the Church tended to be suspicious of sport, reflecting perhaps the Puritan view that involvement in sport was a 'fearfull ingratitude and provocation unto the glorious God'. This negative view of sport was probably based partly on external factors such as the association with drinking and gambling. Moreover, much sport takes place on a Sunday. Sport was also seen as leading to fanaticism, exposing one's body unnecessarily to injury, and also as a distraction from the more pressing duties of the Christian.

Tony Ladd and James Mathisen, in *Muscular Christianity*, quote Howard Hopkins' *History of the YMCA in North America*, which lists arguments against Christian participation in sport in the late nineteenth century including involvement with gambling, that sport caused physical injuries, and that it took place on Sundays and in smoke-filled rooms.

In the early years of the third millennium of the Christian Church, these negative philosophical views of sport are rarely encountered. However, the question may be more related to the use of time. The concept of 'redeeming the time' (Ephesians 5:16, KJV) may suggest that time can be better spent than in chasing a ball around a field.

Sport is one of those issues in life which seems to polarize opinions. Those with no interest in it cannot understand the importance to someone else of knowing what the Test score is or if Manchester United have won. Sport can appear to be a religion in its own right.

The similarities between 'sport' and 'religion' have been noted by many people. Both have the power to galvanize a community and to incite people to fanaticism. Both have sacred times and places—be it Saturday afternoon or Sunday morning; church or the sports stadium. Participants dress in a particular way—be it football scarves or Sunday best.

When the Hillsborough disaster occurred during the FA Cup semi-final in 1989, in which 95 Liverpool fans were crushed to death, Liverpool's Anfield Stadium became a shrine where fans came to pay their respects to the deceased and to leave floral and other tributes.

Several American commentators see sport as the new religion of America. The resources being pumped into it, the amount of TV coverage, its importance to the advertising industry, all give sport a central position in modern American society.

James Baker, in the mid-1970s, called American football

'America's newest indigenous religion… it has all the trappings of a cult: coloured banners, armies of good and evil, fanatical fans, cosmic sphere, even its own mini-skirted vestal virgins [cheerleaders] to fan the flames.' Spectators are not left out of Baker's model. Their role 'is not unlike a Latin high mass performed by professionals for the edification and instruction of those deemed by the Heavenly Commissioner unworthy to participate personally' ('Are you blocking for me, Jesus?' in *The Christian Century,* pp. 997–1001). Other similarities between sport and religion might include the singing of ritual songs, the money spent by the adherents, the fact that each can be a lifelong preoccupation which gives some people their meaning and purpose in life. Both might be said to offer a second chance and encourage participants never to give up.

For others, doing sport is a form of religion. Hal Higdon quotes a Jewish convert to running who says, 'Now I know what it feels like to be a born-again Baptist. I try to convert my non-running friends' (*Runners' World,* May 1978).

Higdon writes further of the 'phenomenon of the born-again runner' for whom running is the most important part of life, dominating the weekend as church activities will dominate Sunday for the Christian family. For some runners there is, in addition, an intense mystical experience in the activity, drawing near to God while running, all the more so when in areas of natural beauty.

It has to be conceded that sport can, on occasions, be given an exaggerated importance. Listen to the TV commentator talking about the vital match, the most important match of the season (so far!), in which defeat would be a disaster… It is hard to remember that it is only a game of football that is being described.

World Champion triple jumper Jonathan Edwards' ability to poke fun at himself and his profession is refreshing in this context:

I think you can get terribly serious about sport. It can become the be-all and end-all, but when you reduce it to its fundamentals, rationalize it, football is kicking around a piece of plastic with air inside it, trying to stick it between two posts with a net attached. In golf you could do the same thing. In athletics, jump three times into a pit and measure the distance and suddenly you're famous! Sport does give people enjoyment and is an important part of life but sometimes it's given too much pre-eminence. There are many more important and serious issues in life.

Anyone who plays sport seriously will find it demanding. There will be training once or twice a week plus competition at the weekend. When training clashes with the midweek church activity or house group and the weekend match is on a Sunday, the player is likely to be taken aside by a well-meaning church leader to be told that sport should be sacrificed if it clashes with church. The Christian sportsperson is on the horns of a dilemma, often coping with guilt and uncertainty about the issue of priority of time.

While the Sunday sport issue will be discussed fully in Chapter 6, it needs to be mentioned here that the fact that so much sport takes place on a Sunday is undoubtedly a major factor in the reasoning of some church leaders who are negatively disposed towards their members' active participation. This applies not only to adults, but increasingly to teenagers as well.

It may seem strange, however, that Christian leaders who encourage people not to get carried away with the amount of time devoted to sport do not seem to have the same reservations about literature, art or classical music. Moreover, those who criticize the amount of time some people spend on sport, themselves often spend as much time—if not more—watching TV soaps.

Should the Christian feel guilty about the time spent in the gym or on the sports field? Is the number of times you attend church in the week the criterion for spirituality? It is interesting to note the following perception of Christians by their friends, recorded by Rick Warren in his book, *Power Driven Church*: 'If you ask typical unchurched people what they notice most about their Christian neighbours' lifestyles, they are likely to say "They go to a lot of meetings"' (p. 375).

If we accept the view of the Sports Councils, quoted in Chapter 1, that the positive benefits of participation in sport include 'greater fitness, better health and a sense of personal well-being, a rounded education for children and opportunities for varied experiences and new fellowship in the community', then it seems a highly commendable way to spend one's time.

We live in a society in which more of us have problems with overwork than with the reverse, and in which people are expected to work longer hours than they were ten or fifteen years ago. Church life can impose great demands on the committed, including all those meetings! In such a world, taking time for recreation, literally 'to re-create oneself', must be a good thing.

To take the matter further, if, as we have argued in the previous chapter, sport is a gift from God, provides an opportunity to worship the creator and gives outstanding opportunities for witness, then from a Christian perspective it is an entirely appropriate activity for the Christian to be involved in. That is not to say that the Christian's involvement in sport will always be an easy road. We shall examine some of the potential flashpoints in the following chapters.

Four

Christian Sportsperson—A Contradiction in Terms?

INCOMPATIBILITY?

Graham Daniels, now one of the directors of Christians in Sport, became a Christian while playing professional football for Cambridge United. Graham was enjoying his life before he found Christ, but now it has taken on an added dimension of meaning, purpose and fulfilment.

One Sunday, a mature Christian whom he had got to know took him aside. Graham takes up the story:

I went to lunch at his house not long after I had become a Christian. After lunch he pulled me aside. He said, 'Listen, isn't it fantastic, being a Christian?' I was happy to agree. Then he added, 'I'm sure now you'll be thinking of giving up your job, to concentrate on the Lord's work.' In that moment my world ended. I was 21 years old. For as long as I could remember all I'd wanted to do was to play football. I'd made it into professional football. I'd become a first-team player. I'd become a Christian. Life was fantastic and alive and exciting. And now I was being told to give it all up because it was not spiritual.

Graham is far from being the only Christian sportsperson to be told that his involvement in sport was incompatible with his faith. There is nothing new in this. The 1927 edition of Orders and Regulations for soldiers of the Salvation Army declared:

A Salvation Army Soldier will neither have the time nor the inclination to join in the so-called amusements and pastimes of unsaved or worldly people. He will feel that to do so would spoil his influence, hinder his testimony and be the first step towards his becoming a backslider.

I am delighted to report that the Salvation Army has moved on in its thinking and has become one of the major participants in ministry at major sports events. In the UK there is a Salvationist Fitness Fellowship.

Other chapters of this book discuss the major reasons why sport is not considered to be an appropriate area of life for the Christian to be involved in. There is the issue of Sunday competition, of sport getting in the way of church activities (see Chapter 6). There is the issue of sport becoming an obsession and taking up too much time, which could otherwise be spent more profitably (see Chapter 3). The most fundamental argument, that sport is unspiritual and therefore of little or no value compared to 'spiritual things', has been faced head-on and challenged in Chapter 2.

In this chapter we consider the fact that competing can bring out the worst in people—the win-at-all-costs mentality, the tendency to a ruthless attitude and to abuse one's opponent—attitudes which have led people to conclude that sporting competition is intrinsically evil. In reality, sport is a gift from God which, like the rest of his creation, is misused by a fallen world.

Ladd and Mathisen, in *Muscular Christianity*, quote from *Young Men's Era*, 27 July 1893, where Billy Sunday explains why he gave up pro baseball for full-time Christian ministry —'because it is a life in which morality is not an essential to success; one might be a consummate rogue and a first class ball player'. Ladd and Mathisen comment, 'He came close to claiming that one could not simultaneously be a professional athlete and a Christian' (p. 81).

However, if you have followed our argument thus far, then hopefully you will be convinced that there is no intrinsic reason why a Christian cannot be involved in sport to the full without any conflict with his or her faith.

However, there may be issues which have to be faced by the Christian in sport, particularly the Christian in professional sport. Sandy Mayer, who was one of the world's top tennis players in the early 1980s, commented:

Ten years ago I would have said it was questionable whether a Christian joining the tennis circuit could have prospered spiritually and grown in his faith. Based on what has happened in the last two years, I would say that there is light on the tennis court, and that there is an opportunity for someone to incorporate Christian living and tennis.

THE TIMES, 31 DECEMBER 1985

Mayer was undoubtedly referring to the increase in the number of Christian tennis players and the presence of the travelling chaplain on the professional tennis circuit, which provides the players with fellowship, teaching a church on the move. Tournament golfers and athletes can also speak of the benefits of a Christian ministry in their sport.

Is there a dichotomy between the selfishness of professional sport and the commands of Jesus to esteem our brother as more important than ourselves? Yes, but it is one to be confronted, not run away from. Kriss Akabusi recognizes the scenario:

I am that dichotomy… Christianity and sport are not two diametrically opposing ideologies but rather the realization that the talent one has is a gift from God for the benefit of society in the furtherance of the gospel, while personally enjoying the spin-offs.

THE GUARDIAN, JULY 1992

A CHRISTIAN AND STILL A WINNER?

How does a manager or coach react to the news that one of their players has become a Christian? The reaction is unlikely to be positive. There may be a concern that 'religion' will distract the player from full commitment to the team. Will the player continue to be competitive or will they become soft? Coaches worry that their athletes will lose the ruthless streak which is necessary to take them to the top. It is true that when you become a Christian your value system changes, but it also depends on the value expected by the coach.

Graham Daniels illustrates this point with a light-hearted story from his time as a Cambridge United player:

When I had just become a Christian and was still playing professional football, we were doing an exercise at the end of training. The players each in turn took a shot at goal. If you scored you were finished; if you missed you had to do it again until you scored. Everyone was pushing in to get to the front of the queue and I was keeping out of it. After a bit the coach said, 'Blodwyn (my nickname)! You haven't had a shot for a long time, what's up?' I replied, 'Just waiting my turn, boss.' He sneered back, 'Blessed are the meek!'

'I now think', Graham adds, 'that I was wrong not to stand up for myself, not to stop people pushing in. Christians are to be meek, but not doormats.' In acting this way, Graham had reinforced the coach's stereotype idea of Christians.

Bruce Smith of Hockey Ministries International is quoted by Larry Matthews as saying, 'Christianity was not really accepted in hockey until the mid-1970s because players and coaches misunderstood what it meant to have a personal relationship with Christ and continue to be competitive' (*Faith Today*, Nov/Dec 1995, p. 26).

However, it seems rather unlikely that any of Va'aiga Tuigamala's coaches over the years have had reason to question whether his faith has diminished his commitment to the team or his competitiveness.

Christians who truly understand their relationship with God and why they play sport will be more committed rather than less competitive. Taking their cue (at least, if they are snooker players!) from Colossians 3:23, 'Whatever you do, work at it with all your heart, as working for the Lord, not for men', they will seek to give the proverbial 110%. If (as was argued in Chapter 2), playing sport is an act of worship, then not doing one's best is not acceptable. The Christian should always play with 100% commitment. The meek need not strive just to be lovable losers.

Kriss Akabusi experienced a change of motivation but no loss of competitiveness when he became a Christian:

As far as competitiveness is concerned, I was competitive before I was a Christian and I am extra competitive now that I am a Christian. I realized that my ability had been given to me by God and there is a verse in the Bible which says that we are not to bury our talents. I believe God has given me this gift so that I could express his glory within myself but also so that I can touch other people's lives. As a Christian I still want to win, but not at all costs and if I cross the line second, third, or worse, I don't have to kick the timing machine or look at someone else and feel angry with him. That is a small indication of what God has done for me over the past few years.

Alison Nicholas, who won the US Open Golf Championship in 1997, admits to changing her priorities when she became a Christian but is still fiercely competitive: 'Golf is now not everything to me any more but I still love being competitive, and winning the US Open meant as much to me as it would to any other person. I still want to win and I do not enjoy losing.'

Jonathan Edwards sees his faith as the reason that he is in sport. He believes that triple jumping is 'what God wants me to do with my life'. He continues, 'I became an athlete because I saw that gift [his ability to triple jump] as being here because God wanted me to use it. I believed God wanted me to utilize my gift of triple jumping.' It is what motivates him to keep going and to push himself in training. 'I've had a bit of loss of motivation in the past few years mainly because I lost sight of the reason why I was doing this in the first place. I keep going back to the premise that I'm an athlete because this is what I steadfastly believe God wants me to do' (Ric Chapman and Ross Clifford, *International Gods of Sport*, pp. 106ff.).

With this attitude, can there be a higher calling or a better use of one's life?

TRAINING OR HOUSE GROUP?

For the amateur—the club player—the dilemma is more likely to come when you are asked by your church to be a house group leader or something similar. You are a good club player. You train twice a week and play at the weekend. You are well respected in the club. Team-mates are starting to ask questions about your faith and how it is relevant to your life. One Sunday, the minister draws you aside and says, 'Jean, we are starting a new house group next month, on a Tuesday night. Would you be willing to lead it?'

Immediately you feel torn. You believe in house groups. You want to serve God in the church where you are a member, but the team trains on a Tuesday. As you mention this to the minister, he smiles and replies that you must decide which is more important. He asks you to let him know your decision by the following weekend.

The more you think about it, the more confused you become. You recognize that you have the skills to run a house group. You feel guilty about not using your gifts to serve the church by accepting the minister's invitation to lead the house group. There is a real tension between this opportunity and the burden you feel for the people you know at the sports club. The fact that you are sporty and good with people makes you a prime target to be involved in church affairs and helping to run the church.

Next Sunday, you're not at church in the morning as you are playing in a cup-tie. In the evening you tell the minister that you can't lead the house group because you feel God has placed you in the club. You feel you should be training with the team twice a week and that means, if you do, that you can't lead a house group.

You try to explain that you are the only Christian in the club and that you have a real burden for this group of people who need Christ. Hesitantly you say that you might just be the best person in your church to be out there reaching those people, where no one else can go and re-deem your club for Christ. Yet all the time you sense that the minister is disappointed and doesn't really understand what you are saying. You are convinced that you are doing the right thing but still the guilt lingers in the back of your mind.

To be fair to the Church and ministers, while the above scenario is acted out regularly, there are many other places where the Church is very supportive of its sportspeople. I know of a church which regards an active sportsperson as 'our missionary' and another which encourages its members to join local sports clubs.

If there are not intrinsic problems with being a Christian sportsperson, are there areas of conflict or, indeed, sports, which are incompatible with Christianity?

FLASHPOINTS

The Christian is free to play hard, to compete 100%, but it must be within the rules. Brian Irvine is a Christian who plays professional football as a defender. He played over 400 games for Aberdeen and gained nine caps for Scotland. It is his job to stop the opposition from scoring. How does he see the line between the legitimate and the deliberate foul?

The hardest thing for me is when I'm marking a really good player and I'm told to clobber him early in the game. I am quite prepared to get in a hard tackle as soon as I can, to show him that I'm there, but I couldn't go out and just kick somebody.

These are the parts of your witness that really are in the heat of the battle or, if you like, the sharp end. It is all very well talking about how you handle a situation but in a match when the adrenalin is pumping and everyone is fired up, that is where it really matters. It is also very important that you handle it in a split second because if you do something and retaliate it has taken only a second, so it takes a bit more self-control than when you aren't so excited, walking along the street or something.

It is never easy but you have, in a practical way, to rely on God and prayer before a game and ask for help and guidance in any and every situation that can arise. You trust that that will help and guide you in the game ahead.

Christian players are free to play a hard physical game, provided it is within the rules. The fact that 'everyone else does it' is no defence for the Christian to offer for indulging in foul play. Dealing with a situation where players feel that they are being intimidated by the opposition, and the referee is not giving adequate protection, is one of the most difficult issues to confront the Christian player. There are no easy answers but the Christian must be guided by the principle of seeing the opponents as neighbours and loving them!

Time-wasting has become a part of professional (and, increasingly, amateur) sport. In professional football it used to be common to see a team protecting a one-goal lead, passing the ball back to the goalkeeper who would pick it up and roll it to another defender, who would pass it back to the keeper and so on.

To combat this, administrators have first restricted the goalkeeper to four steps and then banned the goalkeeper from handling a pass from a team-mate. Is this legitimate or is it unsporting behaviour? Where does the Christian draw the line?

Gavin Peacock has earned his living in professional football for almost fifteen years. How does he see the issues?

If you are winning and time is nearly up I am quite comfortable with taking the ball to the corner flag and shielding it to keep the ball safe while the clock is running. There is nothing in the laws of the game against doing that. When I was playing for Chelsea, Glenn Hoddle often used to make a substitution in the last minute of the game just to use up some time. This is within the laws of the game so I don't see anything wrong with it.

UMPIRE, YOU CANNOT BE SERIOUS!

What is the Christian's attitude to the officials? Is has been said that the only biblical reference to the referee or umpire is 'the man born blind'! A more relevant scriptural principle for us is probably loving our neighbour or, alternatively, Romans 13:1, 'Everyone must submit himself to the governing authorities, for there is no authority except that which God has established.' Bob Hamer, who was a Premiership and Football League referee for many years, was clear about this aspect of his function: 'One of my goals is to bring the rule of God to a situation where it is not normally very evident.'

Greg Linville directs our attention to Romans 12:18: 'If it is possible, as far as it depends on you, live at peace with everyone.' He continues:

Living at peace with officials may very well include confrontation, however. It is necessary at times to motivate officials… there are times in which an athlete and/or coach may need to lovingly motivate an official to do a better job. Once again the model for the believer in Christ comes from the scripture. Christ did confront those that needed it. He was very strong in his verbal confrontations with the religious leaders of his day as well as with his disciples… The aim is to love the official, love the opponent and get a fairly officiated contest.

A CONTEMPORARY CHRISTIAN ETHIC OF COACHING, P. 26

How does this work out in practice? Gavin Peacock comments, 'I think it is OK to protest to the referee but only to the point of not disrespecting him. Professional football is partly a mental battle and trying to make sure that the referee is alert to anything the opposition are trying to get away with is part of that battle.'

Brian Irvine sees a dilemma in dealing with a decision which has gone against you:

When you concede a penalty and you feel you haven't done anything—sometimes that will be a bit biased and you have to bear that in mind at the time and afterwards when you are reflecting on it. If it is a situation when you feel that you have been blatantly on the wrong side of a decision by a referee, you have to show the self-control that is required. Now that is not easy, because to show no reaction would mean that you accepted that you had committed a foul, deserving a penalty when you feel you didn't. To argue about it is equally pointless for the referee will never change his mind. That is a difficult situation where I basically feel that you can't win.

Another difficult issue to consider is 'walking' in cricket. According to the laws of cricket, it is the umpire who decides if a batsman is out. However a tradition has grown up in the game that when a player knows he has hit the ball and is caught, he 'walks' (that is, he gives himself out and walks off the pitch without waiting for the umpire's decision). The only scriptural guidance on this issue seems to be Psalm 1:1, 'Blessed is the man who does not walk…'!

Andrew Wingfield Digby, director of Christians in Sport, has played cricket for Oxford University and Dorset. He has given a great deal of thought to the issue:

The key is that whatever you do you must do consistently. I decided quite early on in my humble cricket career that I would walk and I did that throughout my career even when it was the team ethos not to walk, for example in some Minor Counties games. However, I do not think it is necessary that everyone else should adopt the same line. If you consistently leave the decision to give you out to the umpire, that also seems a defensible position.

GAMESMANSHIP

It has been noted that sportsmanship and gamesmanship should, by literal derivation, mean the same. Yet in practice they are opposites, with sportsmanship meaning an attitude of fair play, even beyond the call of duty, and gamesmanship a kind of doing whatever is necessary to win.

Sporting competition is one of those areas which tests the human species more severely than most other activities. In 1914 James Naismith, the inventor of the game of basketball 23 years earlier, addressed the National Collegiate Athletic Association. He said, 'Few college men would take money or valuables from another. Yet they are taught in the practices of our sports that it is not dishonourable to take illegal advantage of another, if there is little prospect of being caught' (*Muscular Christianity*, p. 70).

This whole area is very subjective and the same incident can be seen quite differently from different perspectives. You cheat, while I merely use the rules!

The whole area of cheating and gamesmanship is a complex one, with many difficult practical issues to resolve in considering just where to draw the line. As Paul's words to Timothy show—'If anyone competes as an athlete, he does not receive the victor's crown unless he competes according to the rules' (2 Timothy 2:5)—the problem is not exactly new. For a fuller treatment of the issues relating to cheating, see the chapter 'Winning at All Costs' in my book *More than Champions*.

Greg Linville argues for replacing 'sportsmanship' and 'gamesmanship' with the idea of 'Christmanship'. He elaborates on the concept:

Christmanship embodies the best of sportsmanship (fun, fairness and being a good loser) with the best of gamesmanship (giving one's best effort to win) but it transcends and surpasses them both.

It challenges the Christian athlete to compete as Christ would compete.

This is the 'What Would Jesus Do?' philosophy applied to competitive sport.

MOTIVATION AND PERSPECTIVE

When you compete at the top level, how do you keep everything in perspective? How do you give it your best shot without treating it like World War III? The Christian's purpose is to show what Lowrie McCown of the Fellowship of Christian Athletes calls 'the presence of Christ in sport', the idea of demonstrating Christ's presence with us and in us in the sporting competition.

Jonathan Webb is a surgeon who played rugby for England just prior to the introduction of professionalism. He played in the 1991 Rugby World Cup final. He describes his preparation for a big game:

During the long hours leading up to a big game I always had this feeling that my false superficial layers were gradually stripped away, until it was much more my true self that ran on to the pitch. Whilst this was threatening and uncomfortable, it could also be exhilarating if you could let go of your fears. Trusting myself was no use as I was only too aware of my previous failures. In the end the only certainty I was left with was God. I never asked him to make me perform well but that he would give me the serenity to accept whatever happened to me.

ON THE WINNING SIDE (CPO)

Jonty Rhodes, the South African cricketer, is another who has clear views on priorities and perspective. Jonty has said that people often comment on how relaxed he looks on the field.

He replies that cricket is not his number one priority in life. 'God gives my life and my sporting career a sense of purpose' (*Today* magazine [South Africa], May 1998, p. 17).

No one who has seen Jonty Rhodes play could ever think that cricket is unimportant to him. It would be hard to think of a player who expends more energy in the cause of his team. What Jonty is saying is not that cricket is unimportant to him, but that cricket and the rest of his life are in perspective.

ISSUES SPECIFIC TO CERTAIN SPORTS

The area of martial arts is one about which some have expressed concern over Christian involvement. The issue, in a nutshell, is 'Is it all right for a Christian to be involved in the martial arts or is there a conflict of interests?' In other words, does an involvement in the martial arts imply a blasphemous acceptance of Eastern religions in which the martial arts have their origins? In a book of this type we are unable to do justice to the issues raised here.

Certainly there are Christians who take the view that any participation in the martial arts involves an acceptance of aspects of the underlying religious philosophy. A Christian leaflet about the martial arts states that 'the martial arts is a spiritual philosophy—even a religion—for most of the adherents in the land of its origin' and that it is often 'the teacher's intention to pass on the spiritual content of his art' ('The martial arts', Christian Response to the Occult, 1985).

On the other hand, there are Christians who are martial arts instructors and who practise their sport without any conflict of conscience. In Moldova, a significant number of people have become Christians through the witness of two Christian Taekwondo black belts.

There are a few areas where conflicts of interest between

Christianity and the martial arts may be thought to exist, such as meditation, bowing and the concept of *ki* (sometimes called *chi*). However, the potential conflicts seem to depend a great deal on the attitude of the instructors, and the practice varies from club to club. Colin Opie's book *Prepare to Defend Yourself* is very helpful but unfortunately out of print.

Boxing is another sport which raises issues. While danger and injuries are present in many sports, the difference in boxing is that hurting your opponent is the aim of the sport.

A few years ago, the Churches' Council for Health and Healing published an occasional paper, *Boxing: A Christian Comment*. The report, which found it impossible to reconcile a sport that seeks to inflict deliberate damage to the temple of the Holy Spirit (the human body, 1 Corinthians 6:10) with Christian principles, concluded, 'It is, then, for both medical and Christian reasons that the working party feels bound to discourage rather than encourage boxing'.

On the other hand, there are many boxers, trainers and managers who are Christians and who feel that boxing is part of their Christian life and a legitimate area in which to serve God. George Foreman, who regained the title of heavyweight champion of the world at the age of 45 and who is also minister of a church, Evander Holyfield and trainer Jimmy Tibbs are outstanding examples.

(For a fuller treatment of the issues relating to boxing, see the chapter 'Winning at all Costs' in *More than Champions*.)

PAYNE STEWART

One area to which the Christian can seek to make a contribution is in sportsmanship. In the cauldron of professional sport, an attitude of 'loving one's neighbour' and 'going the extra mile' will always stand out. In the 1999

Ryder Cup golf match between Europe and the USA, the European player Colin Montgomerie was subjected to some disgraceful barracking by the American crowd. His opponent, Payne Stewart (who tragically died in a plane crash during the writing of this book), first remonstrated with the gallery. Then, when the outcome of the Ryder Cup was already settled and the Montgomerie–Stewart match was the last one on the course, Payne Stewart conceded the final hole and the match to his opponent.

It was a wonderful gesture by which to remember Payne and an example to all who play sport that, even at the highest competitive level, there can still be a place for integrity and sportsmanship.

Five

Does God Care Who Wins?

WITH GOD ON YOUR SIDE

The quarter-final of the 1999 Rugby World Cup between England and South Africa proved to be one of the most remarkable games of rugby in the history of the game, especially for the South African out-half, Jannie De Beer. With South Africa narrowly ahead at half-time, De Beer then took over, scoring five drop-goals in 32 minutes of the second half, an unheard-of feat. By the end of the match, De Beer had added seven place-kicks for a personal tally of 34 of South Africa's 44 points.

As De Beer had spoken openly about his Christian faith in the aftermath of the game, one English national newspaper headlined its match report 'The Foot of God'—a reference, of course, to Diego Maradona's handball goal in the 1986 Football World Cup for Argentina against England. Maradona had referred to it as 'the hand of God'. De Beer took the opportunity of the platform that his success afforded him to say, 'I've got a personal relationship with Jesus Christ. I know he's my saviour... I just want to give God all the glory because he gave us all our talents.' However, De Beer went further—assuming that he was not misquoted in the papers—in saying:

God gave us victory today. It had to be part of his game-plan. I believe in my heart it wasn't just the players, there was a hand watching over us… Some of the things which happened out there today were supernatural. God gave us this victory. I am just happy to be part of his game-plan. Sometimes things happen in such a way that you just don't have an answer for them. I personally feel God had a hand in this… I believe in my heart that this victory was not just about me as a player.

DAILY MAIL, 25 OCTOBER 1999

Jannie De Beer seems to be implying that he felt God wanted South Africa to win. Was he right? We shall return to that question later. To finish the story, South Africa lost in the semi-final 21–27. De Beer missed four of five drop-goal attempts.

Whether De Beer was right or wrong in attributing the victory over England to God, he certainly wasn't the first to feel this way. An outstanding example of this was Floyd Patterson, who said of his defeat of Archie Moore to win the World Heavyweight Boxing Championship in 1956, 'I just hit him again and the Lord did the rest' (*The New Yorker*, 27 July 1957).

There is a school of thought found in some circles which sees Christianity as the supreme motivation for success on the sports field. The following three quotations illustrate the point:

I firmly believe that if Jesus Christ was sliding into second base, he would knock the second baseman into left field to break up the double play. Christ might not throw a spitball but he would play hard within the rules.

FRITZ PETERSEN, THE NEW YORK TIMES, 10 MAY 1981

(A spitball is illegal—doctoring the ball with spit. Taking out someone running to second base, either by putting a cross body block on the runner or by going in feet first to knock the runner into centre field, is legal but considered unsportsmanlike. Petersen is saying that Jesus would not have done anything illegal but would have played hard to the point of unsportsmanship.)

There is also this attitude among Christian athletes: even though I'm a Christian I can play a rough brand of football. In effect, as a Christian I ought to play an even rougher brand than anyone else. I represent the greatest cause on earth and I should represent this cause with excellence in sports. Obviously I would play fair and square, but tough.

BILL GLASS, *EXPECT TO WIN*

If I could put Jesus Christ into my shoes he would be the most aggressive and intense performer on the field. He would win every time.

DAVE DRAVECHY, PITCHER FOR THE SAN FRANCISCO GIANTS

Whether this is the Jesus of the New Testament or an embodiment of a human fantasy is very much open to question. The Jesus portrayed here is perhaps rather at odds with the biblical Jesus of Nazareth, whose kingdom was not of this world. There is surely a danger in this whole area of seeing Christianity as just one more gimmick to help win the vital game. This also appears to be a version of the 'prosperity gospel', a view that God will bless faithful Christians with good health and prosperity and also with success in all they do (including sport). There is not space in this book for a discussion of the 'prosperity gospel'. Suffice it to say, I find no biblical justification for an expectation that being a Christian is any guarantee of success in life, sporting or otherwise.

An aspect of what we might call evangelical triumphalism is 'winning for God', the idea that success on the sports field can also help God's cause. A fine example of this is the attitude of Oral Roberts towards sport at the university which takes his name: 'Just playing the game is not enough. It's all right to lose some, but I'm not much for losing. We're geared up for winning here' (*Sports Illustrated*, November 1970).

I have to agree with Shirl Hoffman's slightly cynical view of this attitude: 'Presumably the Lord likes to see his favourite team win, and trouncing the heathens from state college up the road proves, in its own explicable way, that the Institution's position on theology was right all along' (*Sport and Religion*, p. 154).

In 1996, Alex Dias Ribeiro, leader of Atletas de Cristo in Brazil and chaplain to the Brazilian football team, wrote a book entitled *Who Won the World Cup?—The Answer May Surprise You*. The book was the inside story of Brazil's triumph in the 1994 Football World Cup in USA. The answer at the end of the book is:

It was very clear that the producer of the 1994 World Cup drama was God himself… Although he had not been seen in person at the Rose Bowl, at the closing ceremony, or at any of the other 52 games, everything—absolutely everything—was under his control. God left his mark on every detail. And since he does not share his glory with anyone, the decisive play didn't have anything to do with Baggio's [who missed the deciding penalty kick for Italy] feet or Tafferel's [Brazilian goalkeeper's] hands. Unseen, but real, God won the 1994 World Cup.

P. 102

The book tells the inside story of Alex's meetings with the Christian players, the Bible studies and their discussions. The team had a growing conviction that winning the World Cup was part of God's plan for them.

At their first meeting together in the USA, one of the

players expressed a conviction: 'I think God brought us here so we could win the championship.' At half-time, when Brazil were losing to Sweden 0–1, another of the Christian players said to his team, 'Listen, you guys, we can get out of this one. Our big mistake was in underrating our opponent. But nothing is impossible for God. If we trust in him, he can turn this game around' (p. 61).

The book describes a lively discussion of whether or not it was OK to pray to win. The conclusion was:

We decided that we wanted to pray according to the will of God. In order to be sure of doing that, we would pray that the country that could bring the most glory to the name of Christ, by taking the message of salvation to the greatest number of people, would win the cup (p. 66).

The players' convictions were based on scripture, although the interpretation of the passages may strike us as odd. They had a Bible study of Psalm 18, replacing the word 'enemy' with 'opponent': 'He rescued me from my powerful opponent' (v. 17). When Leonardo was sent off against USA, leaving Brazil to play with ten men, this was interpreted in relation to Gideon's victory over the Midianites with only 300 of his original 32,000 soldiers (see Judges 7). God caused Brazil to win with ten men so that it would not be seen as a victory due to human ability.

But are Jannie De Beer, the Brazilian football team and others right in believing that God wanted them to win and therefore intervened to make their victory reality? Or is Jay Wilson, former chaplain to the Pittsburgh Pirates and Steelers, right when he told the *Pittsburg Press*: 'Spiritually God doesn't give a rip if I win or lose. He's more concerned with my character than with anything else'? (quoted by Dana Scarton, 8–13 September 1991).

THE NEED FOR COMPETITION

Sport lives by comparison. Although many claim that they compete to find their own limits of performance, this can only be established by comparison with others' performances. To be better than someone else is a basic thought in sport. We need competition in order to judge our own performance.

The literal meaning of 'compete' is to strive together. If you were marooned alone on a desert island—an island with a state-of-the-art sports centre—it would be very frustrating. What is the point of a tennis court, balls and a racquet if there is no one to compete against? In sport we need an opponent. Moreover, for the best competition we need an opponent who can play at the same standard as ourselves. Professional golf really took off in the 1960s when the 'Big Three' of Palmer, Player and Nicklaus were in competition. Think how much Coe and Ovett benefited from their mutual rivalry in the 1980s. The importance of competition is underlined by Greg Linville's suggestion that rather than 'opponents' we should speak of 'co-competitors'.

Remember the context from Chapter 2: God is creator; if God made everything, he made competition. In sport we need each other to maximize our potential and we need competition in order to maximize our gifts and perform to the best of our ability.

Christian competition is about striving with all our might but within the rules and etiquette of the game. It is striving to maximize the gifts God has given us in a competitive environment. Will not the God who promised us 'life… to the full' (John 10:10) rejoice when we compete and reach our full potential?

The importance of competition to a sportsperson is well illustrated by the following quotation from Margaret Court, commenting on why she retired at the top in tennis: 'Once

I'd got the Grand Slam in 1970, I had a baby, and then the goal was to get back to number one in the world. After that I was running out of goals. I could have gone on playing for the money but my heart wasn't there any more so I knew it was time to stop' (in David Hemery, *Sporting Excellence*, p.153).

LOVING YOUR OPPONENT

Rather than attempting to develop a theology of winning, we may do better to look at God's purposes and how we fit into them. The issue is much wider than winning and losing. American football coach Vince Lombardi is patently wrong in his famous quote, 'Winning isn't everything—it's the only thing' (*Guinness Dictionary of Sports Quotations*, 1990)

We are made in the image of God and our purpose is to demonstrate and proclaim God's image and presence in all we do. Another way of expressing this is found in Matthew 22, where Jesus tells his followers the two great commandments. He said, 'Love the Lord your God with all your heart and with all your soul and with all your mind. This is the first and greatest commandment. And the second is like it: Love your neighbour as yourself' (vv. 37–39). Another relevant scripture is Matthew 7:12 (known as the Golden Rule): 'So in everything, do to others what you would have them do to you, for this sums up the Law and the Prophets.' We are to treat our opponents as we would like to be treated ourselves.

Applying the Golden Rule in competitive sport is a radical concept. If we see our opponent not as our enemy but as our neighbour, and moreover a neighbour whom Jesus tells us to love as we love ourselves, it certainly affects our attitude to the opponent. We treat our opponent with respect. We play hard but do not seek an unfair advantage.

Our aim is to honour God in the competition. That is our

motivation—not greed, aggression, selfishness, and so on. Some of the practical outworkings of this doctrine are examined in Chapter 4.

A good example of treating your opponent as your neighbour, and therefore as you would like to be treated yourself, came in the 1964 Winter Olympics. The British two-man bobsleigh team of Robin Dixon and Tony Nash were in contention for the gold medal. After the first of their two runs, the British pair discovered that the main bolt holding their back axle in place had snapped in half. There would be no time to have a replacement brought.

The British pair's main rival, Eugenio Monte of Italy, the current world champion, on hearing of the Britons' plight, removed the bolt from his own bob after his second run, to have it fitted in the British bob. The Britons won the gold medal. As Robin Dixon of the British team pointed out, 'Monte knew that he was sacrificing his chance of an Olympic gold medal, the only significant prize that he had not won, by his action.'

Monte's comment on the incident was, 'My action was very normal for a sportsperson. You try to help the other people to have the same conditions that you have.' He still has the mug presented to him by the British team with the inscription: 'A great sporting gesture'. Whether or not such a gesture would happen today, with the greater commercial pressure and obsession with winning, is more questionable.

A similar example came in the 1969 Ryder Cup, the men's professional golf competition between Great Britain and America. The destiny of the Ryder Cup depended on the last match on the last day between Jack Nicklaus and Tony Jacklin. Both players were on the eighteenth green in two shots. Jacklin putted first, leaving the ball about two to three feet short. Nicklaus charged his putt about six feet past and then holed the return which left Jacklin needing to hole his two-foot putt under enormous pressure to tie the Ryder Cup. However, Jack Nicklaus picked up Jacklin's marker, conceded the putt and offered a handshake. The match was tied.

As he walked off the green, Nicklaus put his arm round Jacklin and said, 'I don't think you would have missed the putt but I would never have given you the chance.' Nicklaus said afterwards, 'I just thought, after all he had done for golf it would have been such a terrible shame if he had missed that putt and been remembered for that.'

HOLY MOTIVATION

Tennis player Nancy Richey became a Christian late in her career. She has said that she found it increasingly difficult to reconcile her competitive emotions with her newfound faith: 'When I stepped on to the court, I felt I was in an isolated area and the Lord was outside of that area. I knew hating my opponent was not a Christian view' (quoted in Shirl Hoffman, *Sport and Religion*, p. 111). The problem here is perhaps not a conflict between the Christian and the secular but within Nancy Richey's original approach to tennis, namely that her motivation to win was based on hating her opponent.

However, Richey is far from alone in struggling with this problem. Many struggle to achieve a balance, to temper competitive enthusiasm with just the right amount of spiritual grace, while team owners and sports reporters are concerned that players who take their religion so seriously as to dampen their 'killer instinct' may jeopardize the team.

Bernhard Langer, who would be regarded as one of the toughest competitors in world golf, has a helpful word on this: 'I strongly believe that I can win tournaments without wishing my fellow competitors bad luck or trying any kind of gamesmanship on them.' (And a bonus mark to Bernhard for calling them 'fellow competitors', not 'opponents'!)

But why do people ask this only about sportspeople? The issue applies just as much in business. The Christian businessman faces the same dilemmas about integrity in a competitive environment. The Christian is called to run his business with integrity, to 'love his neighbour as himself' in his relationship with employees and competitors. Yet somehow the question is asked more about sportspeople than about businessmen and politicians, for example.

Roger Staupach, who played for Tom Landry's Dallas Cowboys, made this distinction: 'If you say you can't play within the rules and play a tough, punishing type of game, you can't play as a Christian. You try to eliminate the vicious side of the game but you have to punish the opposition.' Hard but fair, in a nutshell; but where do you draw the line?

South African cricketer Jonty Rhodes is another who believes in playing to win:

Being a Christian does not mean that you have to stand down from a conflict, or not be as competitive as the person next to you. God does not want me to have second best, so I am as determined as anyone on the field.

THE CRICKETER, AUGUST 1988, p. 32

Brian Irvine, Scottish international footballer, feels that the motivation on the pitch must be the same as the motivation in life:

I look on my Christian life as every part of everyday life and for me that involves being a footballer. I look on my football as where he has called me to serve him, to serve the Lord in all that I do. It is not for me or for my football club, it is God that I put first. I do that in practical ways. It is all very well to say that but you must demonstrate it.

Your actions speak louder than words. The calling comes in just being a witness in the dressing room, just by your lifestyle, the way you live your life, just by any opportunities that come up to share what Jesus means in your life. It comes through being in the public eye where you get opportunities to share your faith that otherwise you would not.

Greg Linville suggests that Christians should never be motivated by 'attacking the individuals on the other team. They must never turn competition into personal vendettas' (A *Contemporary Christian Ethic of Coaching*, p. 12). These seem wise words. The Christian must always strive to give everything in the spirit of 1 Corinthians 10:31: 'Whatever you do, do it all for the glory of God'. The Christian should be fully committed to the competition but without any need for wishing misfortune on an opponent.

PLAYING TO WIN

For Christian sportspeople, living our life by the Golden Rule is our purpose in sport—as in all other aspects of life. Winning and losing are by-products, not the main thing. This is not to say that winning or losing is unimportant. Christians do not have to be lovable losers. We do not have to take the words of Alexander Pope, the eighteenth-century English poet, as our motto: 'Blessed is the man who expects nothing for he shall never be disappointed.'

If you do believe that, don't tell Va'aiga Tuigamala of Newcastle Falcons and Samoa—former All Black and Wigan player. He is a Christian but he also plays to win and prays about his rugby! He recalls a particularly tough Rugby League game for Wigan:

I remember a game away to Widnes, in the Regal Trophy. We were losing and were sure to lose. I banged my knee and had this awful pain. It was the pain I'd had before and usually when I get it I can't move. It seizes up straight away and I am not able to flex it at all or make any movement. I remember asking the Lord, 'Only you can heal me right now—the pain and the hurt that I am going through. I really trust you that I will be able to get up and play because I see my role in this team. I see my responsibility to the team.' Sure enough, out of the blue I kept on running and before I knew the game was over. I'd had no problems. I remember walking off. The game was taken into extra time and we had won. I just said, 'Thank you, Thank you.'

THE MEEK MAY INHERIT THE EARTH BUT CAN THEY WIN THE CUP?

As we try to work out how to play sport Christianly, other scriptures come to mind:

'Blessed are the meek for they will inherit the earth' (Matthew 5:5).

'Be completely humble and gentle' (Ephesians 4:2).

'Do nothing out of selfish ambition or vain conceit but, in humility consider others better than yourselves. Each of you should look not only to your own interests, but also to the interests of others' (Philippians 2:3–4).

Meekness is not easy to define. It is an attitude of patient submission and humility. Meekness, for the Christian, is an acceptance of adversity, knowing that God is in control of life. Daniel Jenkins comments helpfully:

Meekness is taken today to be a quality of the weak. The meek are the passive, the spineless, those born to be put upon, nature's doormats… Meekness in the seventeenth century was a quality of strength and the word used is better translated as the New English Bible does: 'those of gentle spirit'. An appropriate picture to have in interpreting this beatitude is that of the gentle giant, a

*large heavy athlete, who wants to win the confidence and inspire
the affection and obtain the co-operation of a timid little girl. He
lowers his voice and carefully controls his cumbersome movements, perhaps even getting down on his knees, so that he can
allay her fears and make it easy for her to communicate with him.
When he can make her see that his strength is under the control
of his gentle will and that all he wants to do is to help her and
enjoy her company, then the strength becomes a reassurance not
a threat.*

CHRISTIAN MATURITY AND THE THEOLOGY OF SUCCESS, SCM PRESS, P. 11

The fruit of the Spirit (Galatians 5:22–23) includes
'gentleness'. And in dealing with a problem in the church at
Corinth, Paul writes, 'By the meekness and gentleness of
Christ, I appeal to you…' (2 Corinthians 10:1).

There is no doubt that humility, meekness, gentleness are
essential parts of the Christian character, but we still have to
work out how it affects our attitude to competitive sport. It
seems that these verses tell us more about how we should
conduct ourselves in the heat of the battle and in any other
sphere of our Christian life, than about whether or not we
can compete to win. Christians are to act with meekness and
gentleness in our relationships with others. We are not to be
arrogant or boastful. Meekness, too, has to be understood.
Was Jesus the 'gentle Jesus, meek and mild' of the hymn? I
doubt if the Pharisees or money-changers thought so!

HAPPINESS IS A WIN?

After England's defeat by South Africa in the quarter-final of
the 1999 Rugby Union World Cup, *The Times* newspaper
called for a new national coach. In an article headed, 'Why
England's rugby coach should resign', the paper's chief
rugby editor wrote, 'Sport's cruellest and most honest trait

is that it has, as its core value and most defining characteristic, the ability to differentiate between good and bad. The existence of winners and losers is one of the key facets in sport's distinction from art.' Later in the same article she stated, 'Coaches need to produce winners... the simple truth is England have been unsuccessful' (16 November 1999). Taken to its extreme, this attitude would call for the dismissal of nineteen out of twenty coaches in the 1999 Rugby World Cup, as only the Australian coach was successful.

The outcome of the game is an important means of evaluating our interaction with our sport. However, if winning and losing are the only form of evaluating our performance on the sports field, we are in trouble. It is a wholly inadequate means of measuring our performance. We can play well but lose to a better opponent on the day. Is there anything to be ashamed of in that? Equally, we might play really badly and win because the quality of the opposition was low. Is there much to be pleased about in that?

Kriss Akabusi's assessment of his own performance in the 1992 Olympic final, when Kevin Young broke the world record to win the gold medal, is helpful. Kriss broke the British record to take bronze:

I had been very confident in the final but it did not go according to plan, for one man ran a fantastic race. Even though I broke the British record yet again, Kevin Young broke the world record. Then I realized that, for me, the game was over. I did not expect to lose to a world record. I never expected Edwin Moses' record to be broken in my generation. I couldn't believe it! But in the end, as history records, I came third and now I'm very happy that I came third and got a medal.

That day proved that I could not be the best. I had to be

satisfied with just doing my best. But Kevin Young and I had one thing in common that day. His gold medal and my bronze each represented the best that we could be in our field of expertise.

KRISS, PP. 7–8

Peter Pollock, the former South African fast bowler, was as tough a competitor as they come. Yet he is critical of the obsession with winning:

Sports fans these days are being caught up in this obsession with winning. More are living such humdrum lives that the only piece of action or stimulus is the match on Saturday. You need to win or be associated with something successful, hence the great appeal of such sporting clubs as Manchester United.

'THE MYTH OF SUCCESS'

Leonard Browne suggests:

For the Christian, 'success' is reaching one's true potential—irrespective of the outcome of the game or life situation—which is important. We need to rediscover what enjoyment is all about for, while it is obviously enjoyable to play well and win, it can also be enjoyable to play well and lose. Success in God's eyes is about participating to our potential and about enjoyment irrespective of the end result.

SPORT AND RECREATION AND EVANGELISM IN THE LOCAL CHURCH, P. 17

PAID TO WIN

This is powerful stuff. However, if you are a professional player, employed to help your team win trophies, can you lose and still be happy?

Gavin Peacock's answer is a qualified 'yes' to that question:

Yes, as long as you have given everything. There will always be an element of disappointment in any defeat but as long as you have done your best you can still take pride in your performance. As a professional I am paid to help my team win matches and trophies. Playing well and losing doesn't achieve that.

So which would Gavin prefer—to play well and lose, or to play badly but the team to win? 'As a one-off I'd prefer to play badly and win but in the longer term if I play badly in a winning team I will lose my place.'

This insecurity in professional sport, the fear that unless you perform and the team wins, you will be replaced, was well expressed by Guy McIntyre, an offensive guard with the San Francisco 49-ers: 'I realize that I'm just in the team until they find someone bigger, faster, stronger, or that they can pay less to.'

LOSING

Rudyard Kipling's challenge to 'meet with triumph and disaster and treat those two imposters just the same' is one that all sportspeople, at all levels, must face. Most sportspeople lose more often than they win. It was Danny Blanchflower who commented that the Northern Ireland football team that he played for in the 1950s and 60s were good losers. He added that this should not surprise anyone in view of all the practice they had had!

Colossians 3:17 tells us to do everything in the name of the Lord. This must include competing and losing. Dealing with failure and disappointment are part and parcel of sport. How does the Christian cope?

Peter Pollock was convenor of the National Selection Committee for the South African cricket team, when South Africa were defeated in the 1999 World Cup semi-final. He wrote shortly afterwards, 'Short-term heartache is normal and even necessary but long-term resentment is as lethal as cancer. Having goals and ambition is biblical and healthy but allowing it to become an obsession—well that's positively dangerous' ('The myth of success').

In the 1991 Ryder Cup, the destiny of the cup hinged on Bernhard Langer's putt. He missed the putt and America won the cup. How does he cope with a moment like that?

At first I was obviously disappointed for the team, all my colleagues, the captain, for the whole Tour, the Continent, that I had let them down. I had missed a putt. On the other hand I knew I tried my best and did everything I could—as I said earlier, there are far more important things in life than making a putt or missing a putt. Again my relationship with God, with Jesus Christ, put it all in perspective. You know the whole thing became too important. When I look back now I realize that there are far more important things in life than winning a tournament or losing a tournament or making a putt or not making a putt. I know I did my best and I can live with it and go on. I don't live in the past. I live in the future.

GOLF MONTHLY, 1991

On another occasion, Bernhard summed up his thoughts on the incident: 'Looking at the Ryder Cup from a Christian point of view, there has only ever been one perfect man, the Lord Jesus, and we killed him. I only missed a putt!'

So often, sport is portrayed as a matter of life and death. Every match is the most important one ever. Every moment is high drama. It is helpful to put it all in perspective sometimes.

Jonathan Edwards has experienced some great moments in his career, notably 1995 when his record was 14 competitions, 14 wins. He won the World Championship gold medal, broke the British record five times and the world record three times. He has had other times of great disappointment. He sees the times of disappointment as times of learning and spiritual growth. One such was the 1992 Olympics where he went with high hopes of a medal but it didn't work out. Instead, he underperformed in the qualifying round and was eliminated. Jonathan describes feeling devastated at the time: 'It was awful... I was taken to depths that I had not known previously.' But he now looks back to that event as the first real crisis he had faced as a Christian, and realizes that it was fundamental in the growth and maturing of his faith:

At that time I thought, 'Do I really believe this? Am I really going to go for it 100%, come what may, win or lose? Is God first? Am I going to glorify him and give my best to him, regardless of results?' From that point of view, it was crucial and laid a foundation for the ensuing years in athletics and particularly spiritually.

Then, in 1996, he went to the Games as clear favourite for the gold medal. He won silver. While it is hard to call an Olympic silver medal 'failure', within the context of Jonathan's position in world triple jumping, it was certainly a disappointment. Again, his reflections afterwards were very positive. Instead of feeling as if it was the end of the world, Jonathan felt delighted that he had responded competitively and performed as well as he could on the day, despite being out of touch earlier in the competition.

There was no sense of blame there towards anyone or anything. I tried to get myself together during the competition and I asked God to help me, but I certainly don't blame him for not winning. Sport is a very up and down business and just because I am a

Christian doesn't mean I'm immune to those ups and downs…

I go into a competition hoping to win. That's the first thing. It is in every athlete to win. So I do ask God to be successful. I don't deny my own humanity because I do want to do well. When the stakes are so high between winning and losing, I also ask God to give me the grace to cope with whatever happens. I have experienced both success and failure and with both I need God's strength to get through.

INTERNATIONAL GODS OF SPORT, P. 114

Losing is part of sport. It is always disappointing to lose but, faced positively, it can be a growth point.

To Kipling's dictum the Christian can add the spirit of Colossians 3:17, 'And whatever you do, whether in word or deed, do it all in the name of the Lord Jesus, giving thanks to God the Father through him.' Giving thanks to God even in the disappointment of defeat is a real sign of grace.

CONCLUSION

There is no reason why Christians cannot compete to win and give it 100% without any conflict with their faith. It is not easy but it can be done. Moreover, because of the great potential for the Christian to be a witness in and through sport, I would go further and say it *should* be done. As Paul told the Colossians, 'Whatever you do, work at it with all your heart, as working for the Lord' (Colossians 3:23). To return to the question with which we started, the answer would seem to be that God is less concerned with who wins than with many other aspects of the contest.

Six

Never on a Sunday?

'Mum, Mum, I've been picked for the county netball squad!' said Jane.

'That's wonderful,' replied her mother. 'When's the first match?'

'Next Sunday morning!'

In that moment the colour drained from Jane's mother's face. She was thrilled at her daughter's achievement but worried by the fact that, as a Christian family, Sunday mornings were always spent at church.

This scene is being acted out in an increasing number of Christian families around the country as more and more sport is played on Sundays. It is an issue for the professional and for the club player, but is probably more acute for the teenager as a very high proportion of teenage sport takes place on a Sunday.

We shall return to that practical problem in due course. At this point it may be helpful to describe and analyse the issue.

THE ISSUE

First of all we need to understand the problem. The 'Sunday sport' issue means different things to different people. For some there is an intrinsic problem with playing sport on a Sunday. For others there is only a problem if the sport clashes with church or some other Christian duty. An interesting recent dimension to the issue is the increasing trend in large American churches to have parallel services on a Saturday evening. If one is in the habit of attending a Saturday church service, then Sunday sport may cease to be an issue at all.

While our focus here is sport, for other families sport could be replaced by music or drama and the issues would be the same.

HISTORY OF SUNDAY SPORT

It is impossible to generalize about the extent of Sunday play in sport. There is great variety from sport to sport. In tennis, for example, most tournaments—including Wimbledon—involve Sunday play. There would be no contract in professional cricket for the player who was unavailable on Sundays, with Sunday cricket an essential part of the county scene. Over 90% of professional golf tournaments involve Sunday play. In Rugby Union, almost half of the major games take place on a Sunday, even more in Rugby League. Club hockey is as likely to be played on a Sunday as a Saturday. The first Sunday racing took place at Doncaster in 1992.

At a time when there are normally three live football matches on TV on an average Sunday, it may be hard for us to believe what a recent phenomenon Sunday football is. It effectively started on 15 February 1981—although there had been some Sunday games in 1974. Now Sunday games are commonplace—often, but not always, to suit TV schedules. Football cannot be shown live on a Saturday afternoon as the televised game could affect the attendance at live games. Therefore a different slot has to be found for it. There are Friday night and Monday night games but Sunday afternoon has become the preferred time for weekend TV football.

Christians who oppose Sunday sport often quote the sporting stars of the past in support of their cause, such as Dorothy Round, the 1934 Wimbledon Ladies' Singles Champion, who said, 'I shall never consent to play any tennis on Sundays' (*The Lord's Day—100 Leaders Speak Out*).

David Sheppard, recently retired Anglican bishop of Liverpool, was in the 1960s a Test cricketer. In his autobiography he stated his position on Sunday sport:

When my faith in Christ became a real thing, I started to think differently about Sunday cricket. Until then I had frequently played in Sunday club matches or charity games. Now I wanted my faith to grow. I needed time to worship God... time to think, time to relax and talk to other Christians.

PARSON'S PITCH, P. 171

Accordingly David Sheppard decided not to play cricket on Sundays any more.

Vic Pollard and Bryan Yuile, who played Test cricket for New Zealand in the 1970s, were others who took a stand on the Sunday issue. On one tour to England, Pollard stated that he was willing to play on Sundays in the interests of the team but would prefer not to. Again, this was in a period when there were significantly fewer Sunday games.

Jack Hobbs, one of England's greatest ever batsmen who played in the 1930s, refused to play in a Sunday match on a tour to India. The match was rearranged.

The film *Chariots of Fire* brought the Sunday sport issue to the attention of the Christian public in a new way. The film featured two athletes from the 1920s, Harold Abrahams and Eric Liddell, who is the historical champion of abstinence from Sunday sport. According to the film, Liddell was on his way to the 1924 Olympic Games in Paris when he discovered that the final of the 100 metres race was to be held on a Sunday. He decided that he would not run and even a meeting with the Prince of Wales on the cross-channel ferry would not convince him to change his mind.

The real-life facts are a little different. Liddell knew months in advance what the Olympic schedule would be and accordingly made his decision to run the 200 and 400 rather than the 100 and 200 metres. He gained bronze in the 200 and gold in the 400. The win was made the more poignant by a note handed to him before the race: 'He who honours me I will honour' (1 Samuel 2:30).

Sally Magnusson wrote:

'I'm not running,' he said, and nothing would budge him. He didn't make a fuss but was absolutely firm about it. The Sabbath was God's day and he would not run. Not even in the Olympic Games… Reverence for the Sabbath was as natural to Eric as breathing and infinitely more precious than a gold medal.

THE FLYING SCOTSMAN, PP. 40–41

In *The Lord's Day—100 Leaders Speak Out*, there is a longer quote from Eric Liddell:

There are many people today who think of those who honour Sunday in an old-fashioned way as kill-joys. They feel that during the years of their youth they ought to have a chance to 'have their fling'. Give me the day of rest, when all the savours of organized games can be put on one side and all life's joys will be greater because of it. To me personally it is a time of communion and fellowship with God, a time of quiet, in fact a time of re-creation by fellowship with God. I believe that Sunday as we have had it in the past is one of the greatest helps in a young man's life to keep all that is noblest, truest and best.

P. 11

One cannot but admire the courage of Eric Liddell and others in sticking to their convictions. However, is it a realistic attitude today? Can the attitudes of the 1920s and 1930s be applied in the early years of the new millennium? Today Sunday sport is so much more prevalent than it was. Dorothy Round could win Wimbledon in the 1930s, holding to her principles of never on Sunday. Today she would struggle to get to the world's top 300 if she did not play on Sunday. Similarly Jack Hobbs and David Sheppard could opt out of Sunday cricket. Is that a realistic option in 2000?

DILEMMAS FOR THE MODERN PROFESSIONAL

Today's professional (or top amateur) sportsperson cannot avoid Sunday competition. If you are going to compete at the highest level, Sunday sport is inevitable. How do Christians cope? It may help our understanding of the issues to look at a number of real-life case studies.

One of the first Christian footballers who had to face the issue of Sunday play was Alan West, captain of Luton Town in the late 1970s. Luton was to play Leyton Orient on a Sunday. The press got hold of the story and, amazingly, most of the national papers ran the story of how Alan would have to miss church to play for Luton. In the end, Alan was not selected for the match. Perhaps the manager felt that his heart was not really in the game—who knows?

Alan did subsequently play on the occasional Sunday, reluctantly but without going against his conscience. What saddened him was the critical attitude of some Christians. He said:

I decided to play after giving it a lot of thought and prayer, realizing that it was my job, not just something I was doing for fun, and that I was under contract. I felt that if doctors and nurses, the police or bus drivers could do their jobs on a Sunday, what was the difference between them and me? It is funny, though. When members of my church who work at Vauxhall do Sunday shifts, no one says a word. Yet when I do my job on a Sunday everyone is up in arms.

Mark Frost was a professional cricketer, playing for Surrey and Glamorgan. He is now Development Officer of the Cricket Board of Wales. Inevitably he played Sunday cricket when required. In recent years the Sunday league has been well supported and, as such, brought in welcome revenue to the counties.

Mark is a committed Christian who was sure that cricket was part of God's plan for his life. He saw himself as a witness in the world of professional cricket. Experience has taught him that being there in the dressing room as a Christian is often enough to provoke questions about Christianity without Mark having to look for angles.

If he wanted to keep his job, Mark had no choice about Sunday cricket. As he put it at the time:

There are no professional cricketers who can say to the captain, 'Sorry, I can't play Sundays. I go to church.' Most captains would reply, 'OK then, play in the second team all year.' The choice for me is play or no job. Despite what some people may think, I have thought deeply about the issue.

I take reassurance from Colossians 2 where Paul writes, 'Do not let anyone judge you by what you eat or drink or with regard to a new moon celebration or a sabbath day.' When criticism comes, Paul goes on, 'Do not let anyone who delights in false humility… disqualify you for the prize.'

For Mark, the most frustrating thing was receiving criticism from people who seemed to assume that he hadn't thought about the issues.

Violet McBride played hockey for years without ever being confronted with the Sunday issue. Then, when she was in the running for selection for the Great Britain squad for the 1988 Olympics, she found that many of the training sessions were on Sundays—so much so that she began to consider whether or not she should continue to be involved:

Missing church regularly on Sundays was a problem for me. I asked myself, was I doing the right thing? I prayed about whether or not I should continue to seek selection for the Olympic team. In the next few weeks I had more opportunities to talk to team-mates about God than ever before. I felt very much that God was saying, 'I want you to be involved in the team.'

Throughout the Olympic period, Violet had constant encouragements. 'While I never seek to button-hole anyone, in small ways I often had opportunities to share my Christian principles and values.' None of this would have happened had Violet decided to opt out of the GB hockey squad on the Sunday issue.

Two top-level performers who have resolutely refused to play on Sundays are athlete Barrington Williams and New Zealand rugby player Michael Jones. Interestingly, both competed as amateurs.

In 1988, Barrington Williams was the leading UK long jumper and also a sprinter. However, the long jump was without doubt his main event. When the Olympic time-table was published, the long jump was set for a Sunday. Barrington decided to seek Olympic selection only in the 100 metres. Against the odds, he came third in the Olympic trials and made the team.

Michael Jones, the New Zealand rugby player, was for

several years in most people's opinion the best wing forward in the world. In the 1987 World Cup, Michael was good enough to play in the quarter-final, opt out of the Sunday semi-final and still be chosen for the final.

The schedule for the 1991 World Cup in Europe was less accommodating. The way the tournament unfolded—call it the luck of the draw or the hand of God—New Zealand was left playing more Sunday games than any other team. In fact three out of their six matches, including the quarter-final and semi-final, were on Sundays.

In the end, Michael Jones played in only one match which really mattered in the World Cup—their opening game when New Zealand defeated England, effectively sealing their place in the quarter-final. Jones scored the decisive try. Beyond that, he played only in a one-sided match against the USA and the match to decide third place, after New Zealand had been knocked out of the main competition.

Opinions differed on Michael's decision to make himself unavailable for the Sunday games. Some saw it as the supreme example of a Christian sportsman putting his principles first and saying that his faith in God—and his view of Sunday—were more important than a game of rugby, even a World Cup semi-final. Others saw it as a waste of his talent, arguably denying his team the chance of winning the World Cup.

He came under pressure to play on Sundays. Some people even suggested to him that Sunday in England is Monday in New Zealand—because of the time difference. Michael answered that suggestion in a Radio Wales interview: 'You can't trick God. You can't muck around with him. It is where you are at the time and Sunday wherever you are, which is the day that has been put aside for church and fellowship.'

Jonathan Edwards, the world record holder in the triple jump, found himself confronted with the Sunday issue at several points. At first, Jonathan did not compete on Sunday. In 1988 this almost jeopardized his Olympic selection. The issue was not the Olympic event itself but the British Olympic trials, which had scheduled the triple jump for a Sunday. The system was that the first two in the trials gained automatic selection for the Olympics, with the third place to be filled at the discretion of the selectors.

In human terms, there was no doubt that Jonathan's best chance of selection lay in competing in the trials but he chose not to go to the trials. The story had a happy ending when Jonathan gained the discretionary place and was off to the Olympics.

By 1991, Jonathan had established himself as the UK number one triple jumper and also managed to beat his own personal best for the event. However, it was also a year of frustration for him. The two major events of the year were the World Championships and the Europa Cup. In both, the triple jump was scheduled for a Sunday. Jonathan came under a certain amount of pressure. However, he stuck to his principles and went to church while others competed in the big events of 1991.

In an interview shown on ITN's *News at Ten* programme, shortly before the 1991 World Championships, Jonathan explained his position: 'As a Christian, God comes first in my life and keeping Sunday special is not so much following a rigid rule. It is just a way of showing that God is first in my life and not my athletics.'

In 1992, Jonathan had a growing conviction that God was calling him to change his stance and jump on Sundays. Knowing that some people would be surprised at the decision, Jonathan took the trouble to write down his reasons, sharing honestly the soul-searching that was involved. The article which appeared in the Christians in Sport magazine and was quoted elsewhere, included the following:

When I learnt that every major competition of 1993 was to be on a Sunday, I was stunned. More than ever, I knew that God was calling me to serve him as an athlete through being a part of the Christian presence within the British athletics team and being a witness to my fellow athletes, and yet here was the door slammed in my face.

My reason for deciding to compete on Sundays was that I knew that if I did not, I would be opting out of most of the major competitions, denying myself the opportunity to develop my gift to its full potential and be a witness in the world of athletics. The basis for that decision was a conviction from my own Bible study that I was free to do so.

In practice, the way I spend my Sundays has hardly changed. I don't suppose I have competed on Sunday more than twenty times in the past seven years. Most Sundays have been spent with my family and going to church. For me, the two essentials of the Sabbath principle are rest from the pace of life and corporate worship.

KEEP SUNDAY SPECIAL

The case for a Sunday free of sport is put by such bodies as the Keep Sunday Special campaign and the Lord's Day Observance Society. In a 1989 publication by the Lord's Day Observance Society, *The Lord's Day—100 Leaders Speak Out*, the foreword states:

Throughout the history of this nation, we have been privileged to possess a great Christian and national heritage... One of the most important aspects of our great heritage is the Lord's Day. In this publication we have listed one hundred statements from leading people, including church leaders, politicians, doctors and sportsmen, who have testified to the importance of the Lord's Day.

It is our prayer that as you read their testimonies, they may stimulate you to make an even firmer stand for the promotion and preservation of this God-given gift which has been a blessing to our people in the past and which will be, we trust, for generations to come.

The case for keeping Sunday special, as set out in *Why Keep Sunday Special* published by the Jubilee Centre in 1985, depends more on the Sabbath principle than on an argument developed from proof texts. It is stated:

A day of rest is part of God's plan for all men. It is part of what is best for man. Setting Sunday apart helps ensure that we make time in the week to rest... A day in the week when almost everybody is free from work is an important way to help family life and friendships to flourish, by giving people time to spend together.

Interestingly, the case does not rest on what is often seen as the basis for the Christian attitude to Sunday. The authors state that the reason for keeping Sunday special is

...not because Sunday is the New Testament Sabbath. In our view it is not... [and not because] it is a sin to work on Sunday. Working on Sunday is not necessarily sinful. Paul tells us that whether we keep Sunday special or not is a matter of individual conscience. Working on Sunday is only wrong if it leads us to neglect the underlying principles of love for God and love for our neighbour.

The authors of *Why Keep Sunday Special* conclude this

section of their argument by noting that while Jesus and the apostles kept a day special in the week, there is no command to God's people to do likewise.

Many Christians today are strongly opposed to Sunday sport. Two letters to the Christian publication, the *Christian Herald*, in July 1991, illustrate the point:

I was pleased to see the letter on the subject of Sunday sport recently. It seems very regrettable that so many sporting events are now arranged to take place on the Lord's Day. I feel concerned about Christians being tempted to watch such events. Many years ago, Eric Liddell set a good example when he refused to run in the Olympics on a Sunday and other sportsmen and women have taken a similar stand. With such good examples before us, surely Christians today should seek to stand firm on this issue.

What a pity we do not hear more of those Christians who refuse to play their sport on a Sunday. We need Christians in Sport to make a stand for the Lord and his Day.

In November 1997 the Bishop of Rochester, the Rt Rev Dr Michael Nazir-Ali, entered this debate. He sent an open letter to head teachers in the diocese, expressing his concern about the increasing number of sports fixtures for young people that were being timed for Sunday mornings —clashing with the usual time for local church worship, Sunday school and other youth services. The bishop pleaded for school teachers to influence the organizers of sports clubs to rearrange their meetings for Saturdays or Sunday afternoons, to allow young people to attend church if they wished to do so.

It is interesting to note that the bishop here clearly aligned himself with the 'Sunday sport is only an issue when it clashes with church' lobby. He had no problem with Sunday sport as such. But I wonder if, as well as urging schools not to organize sport which clashed with church, he also encouraged churches to recognize the fact of Sunday sport and to try to be creative as to when they held their youth worship services and Sunday school. Do these have to be exclusively on Sunday morning?

ANECDOTAL EVIDENCE

While anecdotal evidence is of limited value in addressing what some see as a moral issue, it is interesting to see how Christian families at different levels of sport and from different denominational backgrounds have faced the issues of Sunday sport. There is also the temptation to write policy from individual cases. Take two sporty Christian families: one allows their children to play Sunday sport, the other family does not. If the children grow up believing in Christ, each family will no doubt conclude that its attitude to Sunday sport is vindicated!

A report in *Faith Today* (Nov/Dec 1995, pp. 27–28) begins with an interesting question: 'What do you do when your son's ice hockey games take place on an evening when you work?' The article then mentions that the father in question is pastor of a church! Well, what should he do? The article continues:

If you are Pastor John McLaverty, you ask the elders and deacons for the night off. McLaverty, pastor of Spring Garden Baptist Church in Willowdale on the border of Toronto, had always been involved in his sons' sport…

McLaverty decided to manage the team for two reasons. He wanted to show his sons that work was not more important than family, and he saw it as a ministry opportunity. So he asked the deacons and elders for Sunday evenings off. The church, which McLaverty describes as fairly progressive and open, granted his request. 'Jesus faced the same issue when he healed and became involved in ministry on the Sabbath,' says McLaverty. 'Christians have to be out in the real world. We have to be a Christian in our culture.'

McLaverty thinks he had an impact on the non-Christians around him while managing the team. 'People knew I was a Christian and a minister. Some have come to church. I've also been asked to do funerals for people I've known from sports,' he said.

Dickie Bird (a building supervisor at the University of Essex, not the cricket umpire) had a different experience. His sons were involved in Sunday football before he became a Christian:

When my wife and I became Christians we began to question where we should be on a Sunday, supporting our boys or in fellowship with other Christians in our local church? So we decided to spend time with the Lord in prayer, and we asked him to clearly show us where he would have us be and how we could really serve him.

The following Sunday, while watching the boys playing football, without any leading up to it at all, one of the other parents asked right out of the blue if we were Christians and we were able to share our faith with them. Since then we have had some very interesting conversations, either on the touchline or back in the clubhouse over a drink. Since that time God has been very gracious to us and clearly shown us where he wants us to be— right there in the changing rooms of life. Over the last couple of years, as I have got more involved in sport and its outreach I have seen a lot of seeds sown and I am sure that in the Lord's time those seeds will bear fruit. The ball must ultimately lie in our court, but if we are prepared to spend time in prayer with the Lord and listen to what he has to say, then I am sure he will guide each and every one of us to what path he would have us take.

CHRISTIANS IN SPORT MAGAZINE, AUGUST 1997, p. 17

David Adcock, a full-time elder in the Community Church, Southampton, wrote an account of his experience in the Christians in Sport magazine under the title, 'Confessions of a Footballer's Father'. It all started when his son, Stephen, started to play for Lordswood United:

The first difficult decision to make was when we discovered that the team was to play on Sunday mornings. The tune of Chariots of Fire ran through my mind. Should we allow him to play and thereby miss church? This obviously has to be an individual decision but for Stephen, who attends a Christian school and has been brought up with his life steeped in the church, we thought it was OK. Obviously, though, I couldn't be a dad on the touchline most weeks...

Actually, for someone like myself who spends so much of his time with church people, Lordswood United has given me plenty of opportunities to gently share my faith. It's not been all roses, however. I got myself into a potentially heated argument when opposing fans were accusing a linesman of cheating. Then I desperately hoped that I would not be recognized as a Christian! I learnt through that incident and now try to chat to parents from the other team.

What about Stephen? He's had to learn to win and to lose, to keep his head up whilst facing defeat, to forgive those who make mistakes as well as forgiving opposing forwards who go in over the top, and to bounce back when he fumbles the ball. Travelling with the other lads has given him opportunities to share his faith, and finding some success in football has greatly increased his confidence.

CHRISTIANS IN SPORT MAGAZINE, No. 3/4, 1991, p. 31

John, Dickie and David are just three examples of people addressing the Sunday sport issue. Their experience is recorded not to be followed blindly but in the hope that it may help someone else as they think through the issues.

SUMMARY OF ISSUES

Before moving towards some kind of solution from a biblical perspective, let us attempt a summary of the issues raised. Sunday sport is essentially a modern issue, with Sunday play becoming the norm only in the past twenty to thirty years in most professional sports. This explains why there is often a generational difference of opinion on the subject. Most Christians would prefer not to have to play on a Sunday but if the particular event or competition takes place on a Sunday, then the choice is either to play then or to opt out of the competition.

Some Christians decide not to compete on a Sunday because they feel it would be wrong to do so. Others do not see it in terms of 'right' and 'wrong' but rather as choosing not to play on a Sunday for personal spiritual reasons. Still others only see a conflict if the Sunday sport clashes with a church service. These distinctions are important. If you are asking what is the biblical answer to the Sunday sport question, we need also to know which Sunday sport question that is!

It is also important to understand the issue from the sportsperson's perspective. Unsporty people often see the issue as not playing your sport on Sunday when you have six other days for sport; as you have six other days to play football/hockey/netball, then it is not much of a sacrifice not to play on one day. With respect, that attitude misses the point: if your club plays all its matches on Sunday and if all the county fixtures are on Sunday, then either you play on Sunday or you don't play at all.

Sunday Sport: A Biblical View

Our starting point in a consideration of Sunday sport from a biblical perspective is the belief, as expressed in Chapter 1, that sport is part of God's creation and is therefore good. Eric Liddell's 'When I run, I feel his pleasure' is a thoroughly biblical view. It follows from this that it cannot be argued, in absolute terms, that attending church is better than playing football. (Of course there are the issues of a need for fellowship, teaching, being part of a community of believers and balance in life, which we will address later.)

The point being made here is to challenge the theology behind the opinion often expressed to today's sporty teenager, that in a conflict between church and Sunday sport, choosing church is always better. If sport is part of God's creation, then God can (and must) be worshipped on the sports field as much as anywhere else.

We read in Genesis 2:3, 'God blessed the seventh day and made it holy' and in Exodus 20:8, 'Remember the Sabbath day by keeping it holy.' Have these texts any relevance to the issue of Sunday sport? I would suggest not. If sport is part of God's creation, there is nothing unholy about it. There is also the wider issue of what is meant by the Sabbath.

In an article in the Australian *SLM [Specialised Life-Oriented Ministries] Newsletter* entitled, 'Sunday Sport is not a Compromise', Simon Manchester argues:

I know the 'one day in seven' is a very sacred cow but it is not taught in Genesis 2, before the fall, or after the resurrection. Try giving a new Christian a New Testament and see if they can find any law about the Sabbath—it's gone! But the commandment to remember the seventh day is fulfilled in Christians who come to Jesus and then live seven days in his spiritual worship (Romans12:1).

Simon Manchester also points out that Genesis 2 is often misunderstood. 'Many people read Genesis 2 and assume it tells us to have a day of rest. It doesn't. In Genesis 2:1 we are told that *God* rested but nowhere does he tell the man and woman to rest.'

He continues his argument through Old Testament references.

In Exodus 16 after he rescued his people from slavery in Egypt, Moses begins to teach them about the seventh day by telling them not to work. In Exodus 20 he leads them to the Sinai mountain and makes the seventh day a law (the fourth commandment).

In Leviticus 25 he makes it law to rest the land—proof positive that the 'rest' is bigger than sitting around! In Deuteronomy 5 he repeats the law—they must remember God their maker, rescuer and priorities of the 'rest'.

In the New Testament, Jesus says to his followers, 'Come to me and I will give you rest' (Matthew 11:25), and in Hebrews 4:3 we learn that we enter God's Sabbath rest by believing in Christ. We are called not just to keep one day holy, but to live all seven days in spiritual worship of God (Romans 12:1).

Simon Manchester concludes his argument:

Sunday is useful for meeting to learn about Jesus Christ (and special because it's the resurrection day) but there is no teaching in the New Testament about physical resting or which day is essential. (See Romans 14:5, 'One man considers one day more sacred than another; another man considers every day alike. Each one should be fully convinced in his own mind.')

The heart of the issue is our understanding of the biblical doctrine of the Sabbath. That is the fundamental theological issue at stake here. Is the biblical position on the Sabbath that it is absolutely sacred as a day to be set aside for not working, for worshipping God and meeting together as Christians?

If God made everything and there is nothing sacred or secular, then to worship God is to worship him with all that you are, with all your heart and mind, and if you're doing that in sport it's the same as saying your prayers.

But the fundamental issue is a sabbatarian issue—if the Sunday is a Sabbath in the New Testament, is it a specific day of the week or not? If the Sabbath for the Christian means entering into the Sabbath rest talked about in Hebrews 4:3 (where we enter into a Sabbath rest in Christ, which means that all the time is a Sabbath rest in Christ) that means that all the time is a 'Sunday'. Every moment of every day is a time to worship God—not just the first 24 hours of each week.

Playing sport on Sunday is as legitimate as any other human activity. There is nothing inherently sinful about sport on Sunday. At the same time, the implications of regular Sunday sport clashing with church need to be addressed both by the individual and the Church. It is a clear teaching of scripture that we should be having regular fellowship and Christian teaching. If this cannot be done on a Sunday morning, then another time in the week needs to be found. The Christian teenager and Christian parents of teenagers have a responsibility to ensure that their legit-imate involvement in sport on Sunday morning does not prevent them from growing in their Christian lives.

Equally, church leaders and youth leaders, confronted with many of their teenagers' involvement in Sunday sport (or music or drama), would be well advised to consider whether there is a more appropriate time of the week for their youth activities than Sunday mornings.

TEENAGE SPORT

Now let us return to the issue where we started and approach it in the light of biblical material and the experience of other sportspeople. In noting the predominance of Sunday teenage sport, it would be unwise to see within it a devilish plot. There are strong pragmatic reasons why so much teenage sport takes place on a Sunday.

- *Availability of pitches:* I have been involved in a boys' football club for several years which runs up to nine age-groups, from 7 to 16. With the best will in the world, it is impossible for nine age-groups to be accommodated on two pitches in one day. However, if half the teams play on Saturday and half on Sunday, then the problem is solved.

- *Clashes for players:* School sport is generally deemed to take priority over club sport on a Saturday, making Sunday a safer bet for club fixtures. Moreover, teenagers attending independent schools are often in school on Saturday mornings. In some sports clubs, matches may be on Saturdays and county and representative matches on Sundays.

- *Clashes for coaches:* In some cases club coaches may be teachers who are involved with school teams on Saturdays. Again the coaches may play for a Saturday team. In either case the coach is only available to a club if it has Sunday fixtures.

- *League rules:* In many cases the day that a team plays is determined by the league rules. For example in the area in which I live, the Witney Boys' football leagues are Saturday leagues up to the age of 11 and Sunday leagues at 11+. If a team in the 11+ age groups does not want to play on Sundays, they cannot play competitive football.

SOLVING THE PROBLEM

There are no easy answers for the Christian family caught in this situation. Here are some suggestions for a strategy.

- Share the dilemma with your church leadership and get them involved in supporting you in the decision you make.
- Check if there is an alternative to Sunday morning. If it is the county squad, then obviously there is no alternative—either you play when they play or you don't play at all. If it is a club, check if there is any scope for playing on Saturdays or even Sunday afternoons. Talk to the team manager about your dilemma. It sometimes emerges that other parents, for whatever reason, would also prefer not to play on Sunday mornings.
- Look for a Christian alternative. If you decide to play on Sunday mornings then look for a Christian group which meets another time of the week, for example a Crusader group. Or try to persuade your church to provide a group for the relevant age group at a time other than on a Sunday morning.
- Finally, whatever decision you take, go for it with all your might.

POSTSCRIPT

For an alternative view of the issues relating to Sunday sport, see Greg Linville, *The Theology of Competition: Addendum 1, Lord's Day Issues*. The argument in his paper is that

...any organized athletic activity which prohibits (or curtails) one's involvement in using the Lord's day as a day for spiritual development including preventing one from attending church, or which makes someone unnecessarily work, must not be organized or participated in.

P. XVI

While it is neither necessary nor appropriate in this book to seek to discuss or refute Greg Linville's arguments, the author feels that his article would give little help to the family faced with the dilemma with which we started this chapter.

Seven

Reaching the World of Sport for Christ

If you are a Christian who loves sport, who spends much of life playing sport, if you are thoroughly at home in the clubhouse bar or with the dressing room banter, then does it not follow that this is the world where you are likely to be an effective witness? Just prior to his ascension, Jesus told his disciples, 'You will be my witnesses in Jerusalem and in all Judea and Samaria and to the ends of the Earth' (Acts 1:8). Now no one will convince me that this verse does not include the world of sport!

Moreover, for the sportsperson, the subculture of sport will not just be included in the verse; it will be your 'Jerusalem'. It will be the location of your primary witness, the place where you are most at home and most likely to be effective.

The strategy here is a simple one. It requires Christian sportspeople simply to be themselves. It is a Christian ministry of presence—just being there. The experience of playing sport with committed Christians should, hopefully, lead the non-church member to ask questions about attitudes, motivation, and so on, as well as affording the Christians opportunities to talk naturally about their faith.

The Times newspaper reported a brilliant example of this. Jason Robinson, the Wigan Rugby League player, was asked in an interview on fitness for the sports pages: 'Why did you become a Christian?' His reply was:

I saw this man [Va'aiga Tuigamala] who played the same game as me but didn't need all the going out and drinking. He was at peace with himself. There was something there that I wanted, so I talked to him about it and he explained his faith. I used to be one of the lads and was down the pub all the time. I've not been in a pub drinking for four years. There's more to life than sitting in a smelly pub.

1 NOVEMBER 1999

Evangelism through sport is not as new a phenomenon as we might think. Ladd and Mathisen in *Muscular Christianity* refer to Robert McBurney's gymnasium in America in the 1870s and add that 'the gym was perceived as a means of drawing young men into Bible studies' (p. 36). John Pollock, in his biography of D.L. Moody, the great American evangelist of the late nineteenth century, states that at his boys' camp Moody would 'challenge the college boys to race him carrying enough ballast to equal his weight and beat them over twenty-five or thirty yards' (p. 258). James Naismith created basketball while he was an instructor with the YMCA. His goal was to provide boys and girls with an indoor activity that could be blended with regular Bible study programmes.

Yet in a real sense we are the first generation to try seriously to fulfil the great commission to the world of sport. We are pioneers. The door has been opened by the grace of God because of the massive global impact of sport. There are lots of issues to be faced as we try to give those who take the baton from us a clear foundation on which to build.

The Christians in Sport student work is a fine example of reaching the world of sport for Christ. It will serve as an excellent case study. However, the principles set out here are equally applicable to all aspects of the world of sport and can be put into practice by anyone who is engaged in sport at any level.

Christians in Sport student groups are groups of Christian sportspeople in any particular university. They have a very specific target—the sporty students of their university, those playing serious university-level sport. The Christians meet about once a week to pray for each other, for their team-mates and for the sportspeople of the university. As sportspeople, they are insiders, part of the sports culture of the university, members of the various university first teams. The non-Christian sportspeople are their friends. Quite naturally they talk to their friends about everything. Their Christian faith may come up naturally. Alternatively, after living, training, playing, travelling with them week in, week out, the non-Christian team-mate may become curious and ask a question.

The question probably won't be as dramatic as the Philippian jailer's to Paul and Silas: 'Sirs, what must I do to be saved?' (Acts 16:30). It is more likely to be, 'I have this problem at work. You're a Christian. What would you do?' Because they play sport together, a relationship develops and there is enough trust for the non-Christian to ask for help when they need it. It is relational evangelism, where the opportunity arises for Christians to share their faith, because they are known and trusted by their team-mates.

Think how Jesus operated. The people saw him at work in the temple, kicking over the money-changers' tables. They saw his miracles at Cana in Galilee. They watched him and then they were ready to ask him questions. The people who are going to hear the message from you also need to see the message in you. And they will see the message in you by belonging to the same culture that you belong to. With all our faults and weaknesses, we still represent Jesus to them.

In a situation where Christian players are praying for and witnessing to their team-mates, inviting them to hear the gospel is a natural next step. An evangelistic event has to be relevant. It is unlikely to be the morning service at church—a bit too religious for a first step. It is more likely to be a sports dinner, ideally in a sports pavilion, the bar or some other venue where the non-Christian will feel comfortable. The gospel will be presented by an evangelist who understands the sports culture and who can communicate the gospel in a relevant way. If the speaker can be supported by the faith story of a local Christian sportsperson, so much the better.

Stories involving two of my colleagues at Christians in Sport further illustrate the vision of reaching the world of sport for Christ. Jill Ireland was a hockey player at Loughborough University. On the bus returning from an away game she sat next to a team-mate, Lynda Hewitt, who happened to be a Christian. Lynda shared her faith with Jill. Jill asked her some questions, became quite interested and eventually became a Christian herself.

When she finished her studies she came to Oxford and joined Oxford Hawks Hockey Club. As it became known in the club that she was a Christian, Jill sensed that the captain, Wendy, seemed interested when the subject of Christianity came up.

One day Jill plucked up enough courage to invite Wendy to go to church with her. As they were walking out of church together Jill felt she should say something. As Jill tells it:

Rather sheepishly I mumbled, 'Would you be interested in reading the Bible with me?' fully expecting Wendy to say, 'No, thanks', but knowing at least I'd given it a go. To my amazement, Wendy replied, 'Yeah, I'd love to, I was wondering if there were some books I could be reading to find out more about Christianity and Jesus.'

They met regularly to read the Bible together and after a month or two Wendy became a Christian. Neither Lynda nor Jill did anything spectacular. They were just faithful in living their lives as Christians in an environment where they felt at home. They were prepared to make themselves vulnerable by taking a stand as a Christian. In human terms, if Lynda had decided not to play hockey at Loughborough, Jill might never have heard the gospel, nor Wendy. Because of Lynda's faithfulness (and Jill's) there will be two more hockey players in heaven!

When Cambridge United signed Alan Comfort, a left-winger from Queens Park Rangers, the writing was rather on the wall for Graham Daniels, at that time Cambridge United's left-winger. Alan was not unnaturally a little wary of Graham, wondering how he would react to the new player who was threatening his livelihood. As time progressed, Alan began to notice something:

There was something different about him that I couldn't quite understand. His contract was up, his wife was expecting their first child, he was out of the team. Nothing seemed to be going right for him, yet there was something special about him I couldn't really understand. He had something that I didn't have.

In contrast, I had everything that I wanted. I had signed a really good contract, I was in the team, I thought I had made it, and yet I felt really empty. I thought it was material things that made you happy in life and I had them. He didn't and yet he had a happiness that I didn't. I had never seen anyone with so much security. He knew exactly where he was going. I watched him from a distance, trying to work it all out in my own mind, exactly what was going on.

In the end I decided I had to find out for myself. I started talking to him and eventually I plucked up the courage to go to church with him.

The end of the story is that Alan became a Christian. His interest in Christianity, however, was first aroused by the quality of life of his team-mate, Graham Daniels. Now Graham is one of the directors of Christians in Sport. Alan is a vicar in Essex.

If we are going to reach the world of sport for Christ, we need to be true to the integrity of the gospel and also to the integrity of the sport. If we expect sportspeople to take the gospel seriously, we must take sport seriously.

In this chapter we have set out some principles. We have given some examples from the world of sport at different levels. There is no magic formula. If you are involved in the world of sport, pray for people you know and seek to win them for Christ.

The central argument runs through the book. The starting point is that sport is part of God's creation and it is OK to be involved in the world of sport. Then it is a high calling to invest your life's work in something you love—sport—being there as Christ's ambassador, seeking to redeem a broken world.

Eight

Sport and the Local Church

The Church has always had a rather ambivalent attitude to sport. As we have noted earlier, several league football clubs have their origins in churches, yet the view has tended to grow throughout the twentieth century that sport is 'worldly' and not something that devoted Christians should really be involved in. Furthermore, the fact that sport is sometimes played on Sundays lends credence to the view that sport should be regarded with suspicion. Again, as we have noted earlier, the attempt to dismiss sport as 'worldly' emanates from a poor theology.

On the other hand, in recent years sport has increasingly been seen as a way of building bridges to the community, of reaching young people and of bringing outsiders within the orbit of the Christian community. As Stan Peters, Dean of Students at Briercrest Bible College, has said: 'For too long the Church has been retrenching and building walls against the evils of society instead of getting out and into society where people have needs' (Faith Today, Nov/Dec 1995. p. 27)

The motivation in any church sports programme has to be outreach. As Christians we are 'Christ's ambassadors' (2 Corinthians 5:20). We have been entrusted with the message of reconciliation and are called to fulfil the great commission to 'go and make disciples of all nations' (Matthew 28:19). Sport and recreation is one way in which churches can involve and evangelize the community around them.

Too often, evangelism only happens in 'set-up' situations —the guest service, big crusades, street preaching. Through sport we can create situations in which we can talk to people about Jesus as naturally as about last night's TV programmes or United's last game. Moreover, by doing so while engaged in sport together, Christians are perceived as normal people rather than as 'holy Joes'.

For a number of years now, British churches have experienced great difficulty in attracting non-churchgoers into their fellowship groups. In this age of post-modernity, the old traditional methods of mission weeks, guest services and attractive notice boards make little impression on that vast group of people who have no previous Christian teaching or experience, often referred to as the 'unchurched'. It would seem, to use a football analogy, that the terraces are emptying fast with little indication of things changing in the near future. This has led churches increasingly to consider new strategies. One of these new strategies is the use of sport.

Bryan Mason, head of church sports ministry for Christians in Sport, likes to use the phrase, 'The Church can no longer play at home and be sure of three points'. To carry the metaphor on, it may be time to break out from the safety and shadow of the stadium. It may be time to play away.

A close observation of Jesus' strategy in reaching unbelievers with the good news of God's kingdom reveals his enthusiasm to 'play away'. He met people on their home ground where they were at ease and open to having their needs met. Jesus was playing away when he spoke to five thousand folk on the hilly bank overlooking Galilee, when he called Zacchaeus down from a tree and when he visited the red-light district of the day and transformed Mary Magdelene's life.

This was fine for Jesus, but where does the present body

of Christ fit into this strategy as we have entered a new millennium? It needs to consider how it can play best on the world's pitch. It needs to appreciate that the largest people group in the world is the one that watches, reads about and participates in sport and recreation. To build a bridge from the church field to the sports field will enable free movement both ways and would be both a revolutionary and productive initiative.

Leonard Browne, in *Sport and Recreation and Evangelism in the Local Church*, refers to the 'criticism of sports ministry from the standpoint of the integrity of sport—that we should play sport because of the enjoyment we derive from it… and the danger of using, abusing or manipulating sport to get our message across' (p. 13). This is a helpful reminder. An effective bridge to the community through sport can only be built by those in the Christian community who have a real love for sport.

THE CHRISTIAN SPORTS CELEBRITY

It seems that the one way in which many churches would like to be involved in sport is in the form of a visit from a Christian sports celebrity. It is certainly true that the existence of a growing number of well-known Christian sports role models has helped to change the Church's attitude to sport. However, there are several problems with a ministry based on using such people as speakers.

First, the number of Christian sportspeople who are sufficiently well-known to draw a significant crowd is limited at the time of writing. Another problem is that speaking may not be their gift. Being the fastest runner in Europe, or a Premier League club's leading goal scorer does not necessarily make you an accomplished speaker. Moreover, if you are training in Newcastle in the daytime, it is not very practical to be speaking in Torquay the same evening!

Furthermore, this approach is littered with examples of Christian sportspeople who were pushed by their fame into a speaking role which far exceeded their spiritual maturity. Such sportspeople can feel used by the Christian community and view the whole process negatively. Similar embarrassment can be caused to the Christian world, when a well-known 'Christian' sportsperson very publicly renounces their faith or simply changes his or her mind on the issue. Experience has shown that it is never wise to give the impression that the truth of the gospel is in any way enhanced by the fact that a German golfer or West Indian fast bowler happens to believe it.

Experience has also shown that while a celebrity speaker may indeed attract a bigger than average congregation, this will include a significant number of star-seekers from other churches. What is more, the aftermath of the service is likely to be much more about getting the star's autograph than finding out about the message in the talk.

A better approach may be to consider sport itself as the attraction rather than the celebrity. The sports service can then readily come within the remit of any church.

THE SPORTS SERVICE

Services geared to sportspeople have been held in various locations. The organizers invite members of local sports clubs and attempts are made to make the church look as little like a church as possible! For example, during the 1999 Rugby World Cup, a church in Wales erected makeshift rugby posts at the front of the sanctuary, though there are no specific reports of any conversions that morning! Local sports clubs have been invited to have a display or to highlight their sport in the church.

The service is geared to the congregation, using more well-known hymns (or perhaps different words to the Match of the Day tune) and avoiding long prayers. The Bible reading might be by a representative of one of the local clubs. Where possible, a local Christian sportsperson, who would be known in the local community, could speak about their own faith in Christ. Drama which teaches spiritual truth from sporting situations goes down well. The preacher seeks to apply his presentation of the gospel to an audience that understands sport. Outlines have been produced by Christians in Sport to help churches do a 'More than Gold' service on an Olympic theme but these can easily be adapted to a more general sporting theme.

THE CHURCH SPORTS PROGRAMME

Increasingly since the Second World War, churches have been incorporating sports activities into their programme. However, these have often had no purpose beyond the social enjoyment of the participants. Some churches have run badminton clubs of a rather exclusive nature to which outsiders would not have been welcomed as their presence would have reduced the members' time on court!

Similarly, churches have played football or cricket against other churches, and in some cases church football leagues have been formed. The Surbiton and District Churches league, to take but one example, was founded in the mid-1960s. In addition, the National Christian Youth Organizations (Crusaders, Covenanters, Campaigners) have often used sports competitions as part of their programme.

However, the last few years have seen the development of a systematic church programme of sport as a means of evangelism, of reaching the outsider, and of serving the community.

Church sports ministry is effectively a form of 'lifestyle evangelism'. It differs from other forms of evangelism only in the methods used to bring people within the orbit of the Christian community. Sport is the common ground between the non-church person and the church.

Sport and recreation provide an opportunity for living out a Christian character. However, as Leonard Browne points out in *Sport and Recreation and Evangelism in the Local Church*, 'This approach can backfire if Christians fail to act any differently (or actually act worse) than their non-Christian opposition or team-mates' (p. 6). The fight between players in a Christian league match, prominently reported in the national press, probably did little for the witness of the clubs concerned.

Just how far the commitment to outreach through sport in the local church can be taken is illustrated by a number of churches in the USA. The Peninsula Covenant Church in Redwood City, California, has a gymnasium, eight floodlit tennis courts, a swimming pool, a basketball court, sauna steam room and jacuzzi, all run on a commercial basis.

The visitor to the Saddleback Community Church in Southern California might pick up details of the church's sports programme, including hiking, motorcycle ministry, racquetball, weekend mixed golf league, women's golf league, family sports picnic, sailing, water sports (water-skiing, white water rafting, scuba-diving, kayaking, surfing), fishing, running, bowling, winter sports, basketball, softball and cycling. And that is just one church!

At Saddleback, the vision of the various sporting activities is clear. The mixed golf league invites people to join 'this monthly fellowship with a chance to evangelize your friends and co-workers'. The motorcycle fellowship (MC for JC) describes itself as 'a discipling ministry fellowship of Saddleback Church' offering 'long runs, Bible study and prayer support, social activities and fellowship, family activities, fun and food'. The sailing club has a similar vision, even if their Bible interpretation is interesting. Their information sheet quotes Isaiah 43:16, 'The Lord makes a path through the sea and a road through the strong currents' and Psalm 107:23, 'Those who sail on the high seas in ships, who do business on the high seas, have seen what the Lord can do.' (Which translation is quoted is unclear; the wording of Psalm 107:23 in particular is unrecognizable from the NIV wording!)

It will take most churches in the UK a long time to reach that level—if indeed it will ever be appropriate. However, there is no reason why any church cannot begin to mount a programme aimed at meeting the needs of the community with a view to winning people for Christ, but which is also tailored to their own resources, the needs of their own members and the vision of the church.

THE CHURCH TEAM

Football is probably the most common sport played at church level in the UK. The number of churches with a football team playing regularly is certainly in the hundreds. Churches also run teams in several other sports. In some cases, the team exists solely for the enjoyment of the players as their relaxation. However, increasingly churches are seeing the football team as a way of extending God's kingdom without in any way lessening the enjoyment.

There are several different approaches to the church football team. One question to be faced at an early stage is who to include in the team. Is it to be exclusively Christian or church-based, or is the aim to make friends with outsiders? Church sports teams have been useful in helping fringe members to get to know other sportspeople and in holding on to young people.

Including outsiders in a Christian team is not without its problems. For example, one Christian team included a friend of a friend of a friend in a match. In the first half this visitor punched an opponent, swore at team-mates and argued with the referee. The team asked him to leave the field before the referee did. So much for the witness of the Christian team!

Gary Piper, vicar of St Matthew's Fulham, says of his church team, 'We formed the team to keep in touch with contacts. The aim of the team is evangelism—but we also want to win the league!' Gary has a real vision for the team and has found himself on more than one occasion in court providing a character reference for one of his players. For Gary, the football team is a vital part of the church's outreach. However, he is at times frustrated when some church members see it just as 'a bit of fun for the vicar' or even a poor use of his time.

Another issue is whether the team plays in a Christian or secular league. Teams of Christians playing against teams of other Christians in a churches' league seem in danger of missing an opportunity. While a churches' league is probably a good stepping stone, it ultimately seems desirable for every Christian team to enter a secular league and aim tò be a witness there.

The witness of the Christian team in the secular league can happen in different ways. Behaviour on the field is the obvious starting point. The Christian team must seek to uphold the highest levels of sportsmanship, play fairly, avoid dissent. Some teams make a point of praying together before the kick-off. A few teams have prepared a piece of Christian literature, which is given to each player of the opposition. The leaflet might set out the philosophy of the team and also include a feature on a prominent Christian footballer and a short presentation of the gospel.

An end-of-season presentation dinner—for the league or just one club—can be an enjoyable event, at which the gospel can be shared.

KEEP FIT

In our modern society we have become more fitness-conscious than ever before. This is an area in which a number of churches have found a way of providing a useful service to the community and making contact with outsiders. The vast majority of keep-fitters are ordinary people seeking to achieve a standard of fitness sufficient for promoting and maintaining general good health, rather than people specializing in a particular activity.

The benefits of running keep fit classes are numerous but they must be properly organized in a suitable venue with lots of space, exercise mats and, if necessary, a crèche and refreshments. An essential requirement is to have someone who is fully qualified to run it. (Details of appropriate qualifications can be obtained from the Sports Council, the Royal Society of Arts or the Keep Fit Association.)

The church (or perhaps a group within the church) needs to be involved if keep fit is to be used as an outreach. While people may come to the church simply for the keep fit, spiritual and emotional problems may emerge. It is therefore helpful to have church members around to listen to problems, offer advice and generally get alongside participants.

A typical programme for a keep fit class might include:
- Warm up—gentle stretching
- More energetic movements
- Aerobic exercises
- Cool down
- Floor work
- Relaxation (with short Bible talk)

- Coffee and chat
- Depart

The sessions can also provide a forum for passing on information about forthcoming events in the church. Exercise is a great leveller and helps people to relax with one another and perhaps become more open to finding out what these 'strange churchgoers' actually believe.

In an ideal situation, showers would be available afterwards. However, this is probably not realistic for most churches. Reasonable facilities for washing would, however, be a real asset.

Church Lane Evangelical Church in Stafford found a particular niche in the market with their 'Day for the Retired', which has been running for the past fifteen years. The programme includes keep fit with about fifty people attending. The day starts with morning coffee followed by an hour's keep fit at an appropriate level for the clientele. Lunch is provided at a modest price. This is followed by a half-hour service in the church with Alpha courses in the afternoon. The group has recently been on holiday together at a south coast resort, following an Olympic theme for the week.

COACHING

Providing coaching in a sport can be a useful way of attracting people. A number of churches have, for example, organized golf lessons in the church hall during the winter months. All you need is a few mats, a net and some plastic practice golf balls and the church hall has been turned into an improvized driving range. Others have hired some bays at the local driving range for the same type of activity. Beyond that, all you need is a sympathetic golf professional to give the tuition.

This can be done equally well in tennis, badminton, squash—whichever sport is particularly popular in your church.

GOLF DAY

Church golf days have proved a very popular and effective way of reaching golfers with the gospel. The objective of the golf day is to expose non-Christian men and women to Christian fellowship and the gospel. Church members invite their non-Christian friends to play a round of golf and attend a dinner in the clubhouse, at which the gospel is explained in an after-dinner speech format.

Golfers love playing on different courses. They are used to attending golf events which end with a dinner and a speaker so they are comfortable with the format. The only difference is that the speaker talks about Jesus rather than the company sponsoring the event.

MAJOR SPORTS EVENTS

As described in Chapter 9, major sports events have proved to be an excellent opportunity for churches to reach out to the community. In some places, a one-off major event has sparked the development of an ongoing church sports programme.

CHURCH SPORTS CENTRES

One particularly exciting development has been that of churches building and running their own sports centres. One such centre, in Diss in Norfolk, was opened in 1997 with John Bussell, an ex-PE teacher appointed as the Director of Sport and Leisure. As the only sports centre in Diss, the church has a great opportunity.

John Bussell sums up the church's vision:

The purpose is to reach out into the community with the message of Jesus by providing a service to the community. We offer aerobics, men's fitness, badminton, football and bowls at different times. Over 200 people who are not members of the church pass through the centre each week and we have made some great contacts.

The King's Centre in Chessington, Surrey, is a £2.4 million development which combines the functions of an evangelical church on Sundays with that of a sports centre during the rest of the week. The aim is to serve the local community and at the same time try to show them that the church and the Christian message is of relevance to their lives.

CONCLUSION

Many local churches have found that running a sports activity is a useful way of building bridges and offering a service to the community at the same time. It is an opportunity for church members to invite their friends to an activity in their church, which will bring them into contact with Christians and show them that Christians are really just ordinary people, who enjoy sport and recreation. A church sports event can also be an excellent way for a church member to introduce an unbelieving partner to the church in an unthreatening atmosphere. Without being directly preached at, they will learn something of the love of Christ.

Nine

Major Sports Events

A particularly significant development over the last few years has been the increasing recognition of the potential of major sporting events as evangelistic opportunities. Ten or twenty years ago, the only major sporting events tended to be the football World Cup and the Olympics, which take place every four years. The Olympic Games, of course, have their origin in ancient Greece. This is a useful reminder to those of us who may think that major sports events are a recent phenomenon.

Dio Chrysostom, quoted by H.A. Harris in *Greek Athletes and Athletics*, describes the Isthmian Games in the first century AD in this way:

Then round the temple of Poseidon you could see and hear the accursed sophists shouting and abusing one another, and their so-called pupils fighting with each other, many authors giving readings of their works which no one listens to, many poets reciting their poems and others expressing approval of them, many conjurors performing their tricks and many fortune-tellers interpreting omens, thousands of lawyers arguing cases, a host of cheap-jacks selling everything under the sun.

P. 139

While obviously some of this description needs updating, overall it paints a picture which would easily be recognized by anyone who has experienced the razzmatazz of a major sporting event.

An intriguing question is whether Paul might have attended any of the games of his day and whether he might have been the pioneer of evangelism at major sports events? As there is no biblical evidence either way, it is pointless to speculate. However, there is little doubt that to interact with competitors and spectators at the games and reason with them about eternal truth would have excited Paul greatly.

Two things have happened in recent years to change the scene. First, alongside the Olympics and the football World Cup, a range of other major sporting events have developed: there are World Cups in rugby union and rugby league, cricket, track and field athletics (every two years), as well as a growing number of regional events—European Football Championships, European Track and Field Championships, the Pan American, All African, Asian Games, and so on. The list stretches to at least thirty such major sporting events. Some of these events may have more significance in their region than even the Olympics or football World Cup.

In referring only to major sports events, we are omitting annual sports events such as Wimbledon, the British Grand Prix, the Open Golf, the FA Cup Final, the London Marathon, the Grand National, all of which make a significant impact not only on the immediate area in which they take place but, through television, on the country generally.

The second major development has been technological. Even before the digital revolution it was possible to have in the UK four dedicated sports channels on your television. This means that it is almost irrelevant in which country the major sports event is taking place since the action comes simultaneously into your living-room. With so many TV channels available, an event which may have had an hour's highlights twenty years ago is now shown live for several hours each day.

Just as the number of major sporting events and their impact on the world has grown, the Christian Church has also begun to see the potential of these events. The philosophy was succinctly expressed in an International Sports Coalition publication, *Up for the Cup*: 'Major sports festivals provide a unique way for competing sportspersons and local ministry leaders to gain the attention of people everywhere for the cause of Christ' (p. 3).

The Christian ministry to major sporting events began on a very modest scale in 1968 at the winter Olympics in Grenoble. The first (unofficial) chaplains operated in 1972 in Munich. They found themselves in the middle of a crisis when terrorists held hostages and murdered some of the competitors.

However, big event ministry as we would recognize it today effectively began in 1988, both at the summer Olympics in Seoul, Korea and at the winter Olympics in Calgary, Canada. There was now official Olympic chaplaincy and event-specific literature.

During the following twelve years, big event strategy has evolved. The initial focus was on the competitors themselves and the spectators who came to watch the event live. Later the vision spread to encouraging churches to try to use the interest in the major event in their city as a bridge of ministry to present the gospel to residents of an event's host city. Then, as the television revolution exploded, it became obvious that approaches aimed at reaching people in the Olympic or World Cup host country could equally be applied in any city or country in the world where the event was given significant TV profile.

A point which needs to be understood here is that even when a major sports event comes to a particular city, most people are unable to obtain tickets and so finish up watching the event, in their own city, on television.

When the International Bible Society developed an evangelistic booklet in the form of a souvenir programme for the 1988 Seoul Olympics, it was an experiment. It proved to be one of the most significant developments in the history of sports ministry. Major event-specific literature in the form of an attractive, cringe-free souvenir booklet on the event has now become a central focus of major event ministry.

In contrast to the traditional dull, religious, cheap Christian tract, these booklets are high-quality, full-colour, attractive pieces of literature. They are aimed at the non-Christian sports fan and at least half the content is straight sport, with the gospel being introduced gradually and in the language of sport. An important feature of these booklets has been to include factual information of the type that the fan is looking for, for example, a schedule of matches and kick-off times, with spaces to write in the results. This encourages the recipient to keep the booklet throughout and even beyond the event.

Two quotations from an American publication called *Mobilizer* provide a useful commentary on the development of major event ministry. (The first is unattributed, the second is by Bill Sunderland.)

For more than 20 years believers interested in ministering to and with excellent sportspersons have met to share ideas, receive training and encourage one another. Out of this history have come models of major sport event-related outreaches, multi-language literature for distribution, the co-operation of radio and video ministries and many other helps for local church and agency leaders.

The materials will be available to churches around the world. This is a major shift in Olympic type outreach. No longer do you have to think that the host city is the place to evangelize. Now any city in almost any country can use the mega-event to show the love of Christ.

For the 2000 Olympics, about twenty different Christian resources have been created by the major Christian publishers. These include literature, video, CD, websites, sports gospels and New Testaments (scripture portions with a sporty cover and including the faith stories of some relevant Christian sportspeople). While primarily created for the host country, many of these resources will be translated into several languages for worldwide distribution.

To help us understand how the ministry is developed, let us look in turn at each of four categories.

COMPETITORS

Major sports events have proved wonderful opportunities to put Christian literature and other resources into the hands of competitors from countries in which it would be difficult to obtain Christian resources. It would be hard to estimate how many Olympic athletes, for example, have received a *Jesus* film or Sports New Testament while competing in a major event.

In 1986, Kriss Akabusi competed for England in the Commonwealth Games in Edinburgh. He had questions in his life but was not, in all honesty, actively seeking God. When he checked into his room he found in his welcome pack a copy of the New Testament in modern English which had been provided for all competitors by the National Bible Society of Scotland. Now any competitor will tell you that major sporting events include periods of intense boredom. You are totally focused on your event and you train each day, but the remainder of the time is spent simply resting and conserving your energy. With little else to do, Kriss picked up the New Testament and in the course of the Commonwealth Games read it from cover to cover. His first reaction was:

It was the Good News Bible and it was good news for me for I could actually understand it. The only Bible I had seen before was full of 'thees' and 'thous' and whatnot—words that I could not understand. I read this Bible and in it I met a guy. His name was Jesus.

I was familiar with the name of Jesus. I was used to hearing it in the school playground and in the Army—Jesus this and Christ that! What I had not grasped was that this Jesus had been a real person and that he had actually lived on earth. That got me thinking about the claims he made. For example: 'I have come that they may have life, and have it to the full' (John 10:10) or 'I am the way and the truth and the life. No one comes to the Father except through me' (John 14:6).

KRISS, P. 44

Kriss left Edinburgh deeply impressed by this Jesus and determined to find out more about him. Over the next few months, he read a great deal to find out if Jesus of Nazareth really was who he said he was. A few months later, Kriss committed his life to Christ. Looking back, he feels that finding the New Testament in his room was a major step in his spiritual search.

Chaplains to the 1991 World Student Games in Sheffield had the amazing experience of a Chinese student who came late one night and said simply in his faltering English, 'Want to become Christian—you have application form?' One of the chaplains had the delight of explaining to him how to become a Christian.

SPECTATORS

When the Olympic Games was held in Atlanta in 1996, the local Christian community saw it as a great opportunity of presenting the gospel to visitors to their city. Quest 96 produced a leaflet called 'When the world looks to Atlanta will it see Christ in our community?' Inside, the theme was developed:*

Will they see Stone Mountain, Underground Atlanta, our beautiful tall buildings and the Braves? Will they focus on crime, racial tensions and political differences? Or will they see the followers of Christ working together to strengthen our community and to show compassion and love to a needy generation?

Huge outreach initiatives, such as handing out cool water at venues, running concerts and radio shows and hosting athletes' families were all part of the Christian presence in the city during the Games. In addition to this, there was a specific witness to the athletes, although this was on a much smaller scale.

The Christian people of Atlanta really took the opportunity to serve with both hands. There were hospitality suites on five sites to serve the visiting spectators. The Southern Baptist Church had booths in the official visitor centres, and gave out visitor packs, containing peanuts, a map and some Christian literature. Atlanta International Ministries provided a free baby-sitting service for hotels as a form of witness. An ambitious project called 'Atlanta Host' provided three thousand bed-and-breakfast places in Christian homes for visitors, competitors' friends and families. All were given Bibles in their own languages.

Five evangelistic rallies were held in the city with Olympic athletes sharing their testimony each time. Youth With a Mission (YWAM) had five thousand kids working in Atlanta, of whom one thousand worked as security volunteers in the Olympic village in order to be involved as Christians. Other YWAM people did sports coaching and clinics with local churches.

The Salvation Army co-ordinated a venture involving churches offering six million cups of cold water on the streets to passers-by. The starting point for this highly successful venture was the fact that cold drinks are often a rip-off in tourist spots. By offering cold water free, the local Christians were not only being scriptural ('a cup of water in the Lord's name', Matthew 10:42) and demonstrating Christian love, but also on occasions creating opportunities to share something of the faith which motivated them. Inevitably some of the churches offered the water in cups with John 3:16 on them!

The two main pieces of literature at this event were the souvenir booklet produced by the International Bible Society, *More than Gold* and the *Interactive Guide* to the Games, produced for the Southern Baptist Church by Dime Publishing. Five million copies of the latter were distributed in about six languages.

The Games generated a great number of souvenir pin badges. A very innovative evangelistic approach was the production of a 'More than Gold' badge, based on 1 Peter 1:7, 'your faith, of greater worth than gold'. Some 11 million badges were distributed, many at the Games with, typically, a local Christian presenting it with a 'May I give you a badge? Let me explain what it means.'

What could be more important than a gold medal for your country during the Olympics? The Christians of Atlanta were keen to tell as many of their guests as possible the answer to that question.

Before the Games it was the prayer of Christians in Atlanta that visitors to the Games would also encounter Jesus in the actions and words of the local Christians. They worked hard to ensure that their prayer was abundantly answered.

THE HOST COUNTRY

When the European Football Championships took place in England in June 1996, the mood of the nation was buoyant. It was the first major sports event in England since 1966. The award of the competition to England was also recognition that the football authorities had put their house in order with regard to the hooliganism which often tarnished the reputation of football in England. The euphoria of the moment was well caught up in the words of the official song, 'Football's coming home'.

The tournament consisted of sixteen teams playing in eight cities over a period of three weeks. If this was the first major sports event in England for thirty years, it was also the first event to have a Christian ministry campaign planned around it. Early in 1995 representatives of denominational groups and Christian missions met at Old Trafford, one of the Euro 96 venues. Those present committed themselves to co-operate with each other and as far as possible to seek to avoid duplication and competition.

At that original meeting the following aspects were identified:

• Literature
• Chaplaincy
• Football coaching and clinics
• Events for young people
• Hospitality for visiting spectators

In the event, nothing was organized in terms of hospitality for visiting spectators. A low-key chaplaincy system was put in place. There were some events for young people but the main thrust of the campaign was literature, coaching and clinics. Key leaders were identified in each of the host cities and a committee to co-ordinate activities in each city set up.

A Euro 96 souvenir booklet, *The Ultimate Goal*, was produced by CPO (Christian Publicity Organisation) in partnership with Christians in Sport, the International Bible Society and the Deo Gloria Trust. This was the first attempt to produce a major event piece of literature in the UK and the initial print run was small. By the end of the tournament 72,000 copies had been sold.

An unexpected bonus was a partnership with a German publisher which resulted in the publication of the booklet in German with 80,000 copies being distributed. This was a prototype of a much bigger international effort for the World Cup two years later.

In addition to *The Ultimate Goal*, CPO produced a tract with the same cover design. TELit, another literature agency, produced a series of give-away folders, *The Winning Goal*, a generic one and others specific to the host cities. By the end of Euro 96, the amount of literature distributed greatly surpassed all expectations. In the UK alone some 269,000 pieces of evangelistic literature related to the competition had been distributed.

The Ultimate Goal was distributed in a number of innovative ways. For example, a small church in Tiptree, Essex arranged for 3,545 copies to be delivered, one to every home in the town. The idea was to do a fresh outreach into an area lacking much evangelical witness and to follow up with an enquirers' group if response justified it.

A city-centre church in Sheffield ordered two thousand copies of the booklet to give away, seeing Euro 96 coming to Sheffield as a unique opportunity which might not be equalled for years to come. Ten thousand copies were distributed in prisons. The Christian Enquiry Agency placed adverts in the *Sun* newspaper offering free copies of the booklet and received some two thousand responses. There were also advertisements in the *Daily Express*, *Daily Star* and *Guardian*.

A church in Birmingham commissioned 15,000 copies of the CPO tract in Turkish for distribution in Birmingham, where the Turkish football team and supporters were based. Ambassadors, a football ministry based in Bolton, recruited teams of young people who worked with churches in seven of the eight host cities. The Charlotte Eagles men's and ladies' teams from the United States co-operated with Ambassadors in four of the cities, playing six matches against local teams and taking opportunities to share their faith. At the end of the two-week period, Ambassadors had taken 45 school assemblies, 122 PE classes and 30 RE lessons as well as 50 church-based football clinics. The teams worked with 45 churches and 54 schools and in six prisons, sharing the gospel with an estimated 10,000 people.

In a number of churches, sports ministry came of age during these championships. Regional dinners in Leeds and Liverpool were very well attended and the 'Night of Champions' events held in the same two cities had around four hundred young people and leaders at both venues.

The Church Pastoral Aid Society took a team of twenty to the streets around Villa Park in Birmingham for the Scotland v Holland and Switzerland matches. They sang, gave testimony, used sketchboards, handed out tracts and engaged in personal conversations for two hours before the game and went to the pubs afterwards.

In the end, there was no doubt that the outcome had surpassed expectations by a long way. It was particularly encouraging to see *The Ultimate Goal* being produced in a collaborative venture by several organizations. A significant number of churches had seen, in Euro 96, a unique opportunity to reach out through sport to the community. Many saw for the first time the potential for outreach around a major sports event.

THE WORLD

Big event ministry is still in its infancy. At each event lessons are learned which are then applied in the next event in the cycle. The football World Cup is without doubt the biggest of the major sports events on the schedule. 169 countries took part in the 1998 event, 32 of which qualified for the final stages. There was a global television audience of about 5 billion. The worldwide interest in the event plus the experience accumulated over the past few years combined to make the event an unprecedented opportunity for ministry.

The 1998 football World Cup took place in France. Almost two years previously, a joint initiative by *Sport et Foi* (the French sports ministry) and the Evangelical Alliance of France brought together a range of church leaders and Christian missions. Together they planned an exciting evangelistic campaign, based principally in the ten host cities but also spreading throughout the country. With 150 churches, 40 Christian organizations, both from France and abroad, and over 2000 workers, this was arguably the biggest single evangelistic campaign ever in France. By the end of the World Cup more than 1.5 million pieces of Christian literature had been distributed, including 15,000 sports New Testaments, 36,000 copies of the World Cup souvenir booklet and 86,000 football *Jesus* films.

However, while France was the host country, it was only the tip of the iceberg as far as World Cup ministry was concerned. While Euro 96 had actually taken place in England, much more ministry took place in England in 1998 (when the tournament was in France) than had taken place in 1996.

Hundreds of UK churches were involved in World Cup ministry in one way or other. The most successful approach was showing a game on a big screen at the church or at a neutral venue. Church members invited their friends along. Many came to the church for the first time. There were many variations on the basic theme.

Some churches presented the gospel at half-time or after the match. Others were happy just to have people who do not normally attend the church present on this occasion and did no more than try to develop friendships with them. Some served food beforehand or at half-time. One church not only sold tickets but had part of the church equipped with more comfortable seats, executive box style! Appropriate literature—such as the Christian souvenir booklet referred to earlier—was left for guests to take.

The success of the big-screen presentations is simply that it is fun to watch a game of football with friends. If you cannot be at the game in person, to watch it with a crowd, with the atmosphere that a crowd creates, is perhaps the second best option. Philip Deller, minister of Chipping Campden Baptist Church in the Cotswolds, explained why his church had put World Cup matches on in the church:

We just wanted a way to invite our friends along to share in the experience but also to invite our friends to the church who had never been before, especially men… We want to get people in to see that church is a fun place… to have a social event and also perhaps to find out more about the faith that we believe in.

World Cup five-a-side football tournaments were another important aspect of World Cup football ministry. Take eight church members, get each to invite four friends to play with them, find a venue, a ball and a referee and, hey presto, you have a church five-a-side football tournament with up to 32 men from outside the church at a church event!

Other successful events included World Cup breakfasts or dinners, World Cup parties in homes, quizzes, a parish sports festival, a schools mission, a World Cup seeker service, World Cup school assemblies, a penalty shoot-out at a (secular) town carnival and a football match between a church and the local club.

That the World Cup final took place on a Sunday evening at 7.00 pm caused a dilemma for some churches. Should they carry on regardless with a traditional evensong? Should they cancel the service knowing that not many would come? Should they try to incorporate the final into the evening service? Some churches held World Cup services with sporty drama, songs to the tune of Match of the Day and sports testimony followed by viewing the game together.

The churches of Buckhurst Hill really went to town during the World Cup. Their full programme included showing games on a big screen, running football coaching for kids, an outreach dinner, a men's night, a family quiz night. They even had a football-free zone and a 'seriously female alternative' involving an international supper, an afternoon of music and poetry and a day of feminine pampering. The fact that there are strange people in the universe who do not like sport and who resent the way sports events dominate the TV schedules, creates a great opportunity to reach such people through a 'sport-free zone' event.

Many churches were really excited about the opportunity which the World Cup gave them to reach out to the community. After the event, CPO and Christians in Sport did a questionnaire survey of churches who had been involved in World Cup ministry. The following comments were included in the responses received.

- The World Cup may have revolutionized the way our church leaders think of the church as just a Sunday meeting place.
- This was a wonderful opportunity to open our church premises to folk who generally would not come to services and for them to feel at ease.
- The *To Be the Best* booklet was a marvellous way of passing on the gospel message without appearing to be a Bible-basher and frightening people off, especially those who in the past have said they had no time or interest for God or church.
- The World Cup was a big common denominator between the church and Mr and Mrs Punter on the street. It was an excellent means of reaching out to others keenly interested in the World Cup with the challenge of the gospel.

Incredibly, in over 100 countries there was some kind of World Cup-related evangelism. For the first time a concerted effort was made to develop a range of World Cup evangelistic materials, such as a football edition of the *Jesus* film, a video called *Will Brazil Do It Again?*, sports New Testaments and the booklet *To Be the Best*, and to make them available around the world. We have space, here, to do no more than give a few glimpses of how the churches operated in countries around the world.

- In Argentina, 400 churches were involved in a campaign for praying for the World Cup. In addition there was literature, video and door-to-door World Cup evangelism.
- In Bangladesh, over 300 churches were involved in World Cup ministry including football matches, special sports services, video and literature. Over 80,000 pieces of World Cup evangelistic literature were distributed

in a collaborative venture between the Bangladesh Sports Coalition, the Bible Society and five major denominations.

- In Bulgaria, 12,000 *To Be the Best* booklets were distributed by six major denominations and three missions, along with the *Jesus* film.
- In Egypt, a massive World Cup outreach campaign involved 800 churches and used video, literature, camps, big-screen showings and sports days.
- In Germany there were some 300 church World Cup parties around big matches, which proved very successful in getting people with no church connections into the church community for the first time.
- Other countries where there was some football World Cup outreach included Burma, India, Iraq, Japan, Jordan, Morocco, South Africa, Sri Lanka, Thailand and Zimbabwe. All over the world churches were seeing, often for the first time, the potential of outreach using interest in a major sports event to create a bridge for ministry.

The 1999 cricket World Cup was another event which broke new ground in major event ministry. It took place in England from 14 May to 20 June 1999. Forty-two matches took place at 17 locations in England, with five matches being played in Scotland, Wales, Ireland and Holland. The following 12 countries competed: Australia, Bangladesh, England, India, Kenya, New Zealand, Pakistan, Scotland, South Africa, Sri Lanka, West Indies, Zimbabwe, with Australia the eventual winners.

Ministry took place in ten countries, principally in the Indian sub-continent. A good example of the international partnership which now exists is the fact that while the Christians in Sport/CPO Cricket World Cup booklet,

Cricket—A Different Spin, sold only six thousand in the UK, over 250,000 were distributed free in eight languages in India, Pakistan, Bangladesh, Nepal and Sri Lanka.

An estimated 1.3 million people in the Indian sub-continent were reached with the gospel in some form through the cricket World Cup. The range of different activities was extensive—122 cricket tournaments, ten coaching clinics, quiz competitions, big screen projections, literature distribution and TV slots.

In Bangladesh alone, there were cricket tournaments, a designated World Cup Sunday observed in hundreds of churches, training and vision-sharing meetings, posters, handbills and several different pieces of literature. Elgin Saha of the Bangladesh Sports Coalition said of the campaign:

We are thankful to God for giving us this opportunity of sports ministry. In the context of an Islamic country this event gave us a great opportunity to train the Christian leaders to preach the gospel. We are equally thankful to our generous donors who shared their gifts being our partners in Christ.

Without question, the 1999 cricket World Cup was the biggest evangelistic effort in cricket that has so far taken place. The ministry was particularly effective in countries where cricket is the top sport. While in England the cricket World Cup ministry was no more than a tenth the size of the 1998 football World Cup ministry, mirroring the relative interest in the two sports, in the Indian sub-continent the ministry opportunities and activities were vast.

Ministry around the Superbowl—American Football's equivalent of the FA Cup final (for the uninitiated)—has developed continuously over the past few years. The concept is simple—the Superbowl Party. This can take place in a home, in a church or a school hall. Church members invite their friends along for an afternoon of food and fun around the Superbowl.

As the Superbowl lasts up to three hours in a stop-start format, the intensity of viewing is less than that required for an event such as the FA Cup final. This enables those present to go in and out for food and drinks—or a chat—during the game.

Sports Spectrum, a Christian resource agency in the USA, in partnership with other agencies, produces a Superbowl ministry kit for churches. The kit includes a poster to advertise the event, along with a video with testimonies of American Football players (possibly some of whom are playing in the Superbowl) to be shown before the game or at half-time, as well as some Superbowl-related evangelistic literature. Up to 2000 Superbowl kits are distributed each year and over 1.8 million people have been reached through Superbowl-related ministry.

Christian ministry around major sports events is a relatively recent thing. However, it is already proving to be an effective aspect of the outreach activities of thousands of churches in many countries. The concept is simple—using the interest in a major sports event to create a bridge for ministry.

The type of ministry is very flexible, according to the local situation and the aims of the local organizers. What cannot be denied is that major sports event ministry is an excellent way of drawing people into a Christian community for the first time and of helping them to find faith in Christ.

CONCLUSION

The message of this book is that sport is part of God's creation and as such is to be enjoyed by his creation. We can do no better than to repeat the words attributed to Eric

Liddell, 'God made me for a purpose but he also made me fast, and when I run I feel his pleasure.'

Sport is an area of life about which people become passionate. It is most definitely more than a game. At times the result of one match takes on an importance out of all proportion to its real significance. With so much at stake, it is hardly surprising that the 'win at all costs' mentality has been allowed not only to raise its ugly head, but to be nurtured and encouraged by players and coaches alike. Sportsmen and women are just ordinary people. They are not the superheroes and demi-gods that we like to make them. They are no better and no worse than anyone else, with the proviso only that they experience many of the successes and pressures of life at a younger age than do the captains of industry, for example. Moreover, top sportspeople live their lives in the goldfish bowl environment which means that the slightest slip is a public slip.

The relationship between sport and Christianity is a complex one. Some of the claims about how Jesus would have reacted in a particular baseball situation may make us cringe. The hope and prayer of the Christians in Sport movement is to see more and more top sportspeople living consistent godly lives in the cauldron of professional sport, seeking to take seriously the teaching of Jesus and to work out its implications in the situations that they meet. In this way they will give glory to God and be a witness among their peers.

Similarly we long to see, at grass-roots level, Christian players in their clubs making an impact by the way they conduct themselves. We want to see every church having a sports programme, seeing how sport can be used to fulfil the great commission of making disciples of all nations.

If this book can help even a little in the fulfilment of these goals, it will have been worthwhile.

Resources

BOOKS

Ric Chapman and Ross Clifford, *International Gods of Sport*, Strand, 1999

N.P. Grubb, *C.T. Studd*, Lutterworth, 1933

Shirl J. Hoffman (ed.), *Sport and Religion*, Human Kinetics Books, 1992

Brian Irvine, *What a Difference a Day Makes*, Mainstream, 1996

Tony Ladd and James Mathisen, *Muscular Christianity*, Baker Books, 1999

Sally Magnusson, *The Flying Scotsman*, Quartet, 1981

Colin Opie, *Prepare to Defend Yourself*, Kingsway, 1987

Alex Ribeiro, *Who Won the World Cup?—The Answer May Surprise You*, Riverside International, 1996

Helmfried Riecker, *Warm Up*, Hähssler, Germany, 1998

David Sheppard, *Parson's Pitch*, Hodder, 1964

The Lord's Day—100 Leaders Speak Out, Lord's Day Observance Society

Stuart Weir, *Kriss*, HarperCollins, 1996

Stuart Weir, *More than Champions: Sportstars' Secrets of Success*, HarperCollins, 1993

BOOKLETS

Leonard Browne, *Sport and Recreation and Evangelism in the Local Church*, Grove Books, 1991

On the Winning Side, Christian Publicity Organization, 1999

The Ultimate Goal, Christian Publicity Organization, 1996

Up for the Cup, International Sports Coalition, 1996

Why Keep Sunday Special, The Jubilee Centre, 1985

Greg Linville, *Athletics in the First Century*, Overwhelming Victory Ministries, Canton, Ohio

Greg Linville, A *Contemporary Christian Ethic of Coaching,* Overwhelming Victory Ministries, Canton, Ohio

Greg Linville, *The Theology of Competition*, Overwhelming Victory Ministries, Canton, Ohio

The Case for Sport, UK Sports Councils, 1991

ARTICLES

Peter Pollock, 'The myth of success', *Today*, September 1999

VIDEOS

Faith and Cricket, Jesus Film Project, 1999

More than a Game, CTA and Christians in Sport, 1998

More than Champions, CTA and Christians in Sport, 1996

INDEX OF NAMES